perspectives
ON DESIGN
NEW ENGLAND

Published by

PANACHE
P A N A C H E   P A R T N E R S

Panache Partners, LLC
1424 Gables Court
Plano, TX 75075
469.246.6060
Fax: 469.246.6062
www.panache.com

Publishers: Brian G. Carabet and John A. Shand

Printed in Malaysia

Distributed by Independent Publishers Group
800.888.4741

PUBLISHER'S DATA

Perspectives on Design New England

Library of Congress Control Number: 2009939299

ISBN 13: 978-1-933415-57-4
ISBN 10: 1-933415-57-6

First Printing 2010

10 9 8 7 6 5 4 3 2 1

Right: The Classic Group, page 73

Previous Page: Meyer & Meyer Architecture and Interiors, page 25

perspectives
ON DESIGN
NEW ENGLAND

creative ideas shared by leading design professionals

introduction

Y F I Custom Homes, page 113

Creating the spaces in which we live and achieving the beauty we desire can be a daunting quest—a quest that is as diverse as each of our unique personalities. For some, it may be serene hardscaped gardens; for others it may be opulent marble entryways. Aspiring chefs may find a kitchen boasting the finest in technology their true sanctuary.

Perspectives on Design New England is a pictorial journey, from conceptualizing your dream home, to putting together the finishing touches, to creating an outdoor oasis. Alongside the phenomenal photography, you will have a rare insight to how these tastemakers achieve such works of art and be inspired by their personal perspectives on design.

Within these pages, the region's finest artisans will share their wisdom, experience, and talent. It is the collaboration between these visionaries and the outstanding pride and craftsmanship of the products showcased that together achieve the remarkable. Learn from leaders in the industry about the aesthetic of a finely crafted sofa, or how appropriate lighting can dramatically change the appearance of a room.

Whether your dream is to have a new home or one that has been redesigned to suit your lifestyle, *Perspectives on Design New England* will be both an enjoyable journey and a source of motivation.

chapter one: the concept

chapter two: the structure

chapter three: elements of structure

contents

chapter four: elements of design

chapter five: living the elements

"All elements conspire to create a home that is serene, understated, and welcoming."

—Susan Symonds

Landry & Arcari, page 179

Shope Reno Wharton Architecture, page 35

Susan Symonds Interior Design, page 167

Kirby Perkins Construction, page 93

Blazing Design, page 139

Cara-Donna Copper and Slate Co., page 129

Bacco, Inc., page 63

"A satisfaction exists
in homebuilding from
leaving a legacy that will
endure through many
generations."

—Glenn Farrell

The Vermont landscape is a tapestry of ancient mountains and hardwood forests, stone walls and working farms. Growing from these roots, Birdseye Architecture and Building strikes a unique balance between innovation and tradition, structure and nature. Each Birdseye home reflects the landscapes and communities in which the home is built and benefits from the company's pioneering role in green energy and sustainable building in Vermont.

Birdseye's architectural studio is led by Brian J. Mac, AIA. With a keen awareness of our increasingly fragile environment, the Birdseye team artfully embraces practicality and sustainability. The award-winning work draws on a range of design styles and traditions, bringing to life the vision of each client.

Located in the company's restored 1880s barn, the Birdseye architectural team works alongside other Birdseye artisans, including carpenters, woodworkers, and blacksmiths. This open workshop environment fuels collaboration and a dynamic design process, which results in one-of-a-kind creations of beauty and originality.

"Unique, soulful, sustainable homes are a gift from one generation to another."

—Brian J. Mac

BIRDSEYE DESIGN

"Successful design is about context, about what you're looking at as well as what's looking at you."

—Brian J. Mac

ABOVE: The design responds to the surrounding mountains with high, steep roof peaks and cantilevered forms supported by heavy timber brackets, columns, and beams.
Photograph by Susan Teare

FACING PAGE TOP: Overlooking Lake Champlain from a high bluff, the primary architectural feature is the expressive structure of steel and glass, which was designed for maximum view and interior openness.
Photograph by Birdseye Design

FACING PAGE BOTTOM: From the low, cedar shingle roof with its copper snow belt to the grounded central stone chimney and the deep porch, each element captures the proper scale for the house.
Photograph by Birdseye Design

PREVIOUS PAGES: The working horse stable is located in the unique pastoral landscape of Shelburne Farms, which was designed by the father of American landscape architecture, Frederick Law Olmsted.
Photograph by Susan Teare

"The relationship between the architect and homeowner is an integral part of the creative process."

—Brian J. Mac

ABOVE & FACING PAGE: After searching across New England and New York, the perfect barn was found in Ryegate, Vermont, only 60 miles from the new building site. We disassembled the barn and re-cut and repaired the frame. The barn was resurrected into a guest house with a professional recording studio in the lower walk-out level. A combination of plaster and salvaged barn board wall finishes and carefully designed fenestration create an interior that is both rustic and refined. The slate roof, restored cupola, and stone foundation reinforce the simple nature of the barn.
Photographs by Susan Teare

"Designing and creating unique homes involves careful listening, effective communicating, and a passion for understanding a person's relationship to the home."

—Brian J. Mac

ABOVE LEFT: The vibrancy of the recycled glass wall is used to define the wet zone in the curvilinear master bath. The continuity of design and the warmth of reclaimed cypress and local maple and ash create a peaceful environment.
Photograph by Gary Hall Photography

ABOVE RIGHT: The custom entry door is built with reclaimed cypress and salvaged redwood. Salvaged granite flooring and re-sawn Douglas fir timber frame cut-offs create intriguing patterns on the walls and floor.
Photograph by Birdseye Design

FACING PAGE TOP: In response to the owner's commitment to sustainable living on an organic farm, a 15-kilowatt photovoltaic array was installed on the barn roof. Solar thermal panels for domestic hot water were located on the south wall and were combined with an extensive infrastructure of wood gasifiers and hot water storage tanks to provide energy for the farm.
Photograph by Birdseye Design

FACING PAGE BOTTOM: A masonry heater, serving as a thermal mass for wood-fired heating, anchors the central living room with a local granite and soapstone surround. Other local materials include site-cut and -milled maple and cherry.
Photograph by Birdseye Design

"Architecture seeks to elevate the pleasures and experiences of the spaces we occupy."

—Brian J. Mac

ABOVE: In a contemporary addition to an 1840s farmhouse, appropriate scale and proportion create a cohesive flow between old and new. The entry porch is designed to transcend the timeline between the two structures.
Photograph by Susan Teare

FACING PAGE TOP: Drawing upon classic farmstead compositions in which the house and barn are attached through a series of interwoven structures, the gracious home was designed for an extended family.
Photograph by Birdseye Design

FACING PAGE BOTTOM: The window details create a lantern effect and accentuate the transparency of the building's corners. The simple roof form and cantilevered dormers add a unique expression to the structure's minimal form.
Photograph by Susan Teare

When is a picture really worth a thousand words; when it captures an ideal, a vision, a goal? For Meyer & Meyer, projects vary in style and scale, but homeowner satisfaction is always the first priority. John I. Meyer Jr., AIA, Laura Brooks Meyer, IIDA, and their team approach each project with a fresh, imaginative eye and explore it from all angles. Each creation shares a distinctive elegance, harmony, and serenity with its surroundings and is designed to last for centuries and be cherished for its character and grace.

John uses his artistic skill to create expressive, hand-drawn renderings. His unique ability draws clients directly into the excitement of the design process. As their ideas are brought to life, clients become active members of the design team. John's images allow them to see exactly what they've imagined with remarkable clarity. When every architectural and interior design detail can be studied, there are no surprises, last-minute changes, or regrets. The collection of images and ultra-realistic models then becomes a treasured keepsake.

Meyer & Meyer's process is collaborative and dynamic. Since 1980 the firm has earned an impeccable reputation for design, detailing, and the use of quality materials in conjunction with the best construction methods.

"Inspiring designs require a dash of sophistication, a touch of whimsy, and an abundance of imagination."

—John I. Meyer Jr.

MEYER & MEYER ARCHITECTURE AND INTERIORS

"We work hard with our clients to discover and refine the most beautiful expression of their values, their program, and their setting."

—John I. Meyer Jr.

ABOVE: For us, nothing is too customized. We created exactly what the homeowners envisioned for their Westchester County, New York, residence. This award-winning project captures the look and feel of a country manor home, but we designed within the parameters of a modern American program. The grounds' highlights include a Moorish fountain amongst English gardens. An underground walkway connects the home to a natatorium.
Photograph by Bedford Photo-Graphics

FACING PAGE: Highly decorative architectural elements transformed a previously dark paneled entry into a sophisticated music hall.
Photograph by Bruce Buck

PREVIOUS PAGES: Neatly tucked into the landscape, the enchanting warming hut is sheer magic. It stands on a small island surrounded by three bodies of water: one for trout fishing, one for ice skating, and one that is enjoyed as a natural reflecting pool. The house features a southern-facing stone terrace and an outdoor fireplace.
Photograph by Robert Benson

"Working with people who love what they do—true craftsmen—is integral to creating successful architecture. It always shows through in the finished project."

—Laura Brooks Meyer

ABOVE: We completely renovated the 18,000-square-foot Georgian estate, built in 1929. All of our work restored the architecture and gave elegance to the once-simple interior. A new limestone portico with a balustrade railing supported by elaborately carved columns off the home's west wing was added along with a custom reception hall, main stairway, and an award-winning master suite. Many people have the impression that good craftsmen are a thing of the past, but this Georgian estate is proof that it just isn't so.

FACING PAGE: The ornately designed bronze doors offer an immediate glimpse of the artistry and refinement found throughout the magnificent home. Glamour and grandeur are reflected in every detail of the home's custom interiors.
Photographs by Bruce Buck

ABOVE: A significant challenge in renovating three contiguous Boston brownstones was the addition of a luxurious 2,500-square-foot penthouse spanning all three buildings with an outdoor kitchen and whirlpool on the roof deck.
Photograph by Boston Virtual Imaging

RIGHT: We have no signature style; refined design elements transcend all architectural metaphors. Classic detailing is at home in both contemporary and traditional settings.
Photograph by Björg Magnea

FACING PAGE: Multiple units were combined to create a 4,600-square-foot Asian-inspired residence located in Greenwich Village, New York. The design takes advantage of the large expanses of windows with galleries providing long vistas to a sequence of formal spaces broken up by custom shoji screens.
Photograph by Björg Magnea

LEFT: A refined country home demonstrates that good design isn't exclusively reserved for the rich and famous. Simple and quiet with an organic quality, the house features reclaimed materials—a precocious inclusion at the time.
Photograph by Peter Margonelli

BELOW: The landmark Stanford White house underwent an extensive renovation including a substantial three-story addition and a new five-car showroom-style garage. The garage features an award-winning green roof and bluestone terrace, providing reduction of air pollution, controlling heating and cooling costs, and absorbing storm water runoff.
Photograph by Anton Grassl

FACING PAGE: We seek resources and craftsmen both locally and from around the world. The charming and unique fireplace was hand carved in Budapest from an original design by John Meyer. By contrast, reclaimed antique timber beams provide structural and decorative elements within the warming hut.
Photograph by Robert Benson

Bernard Wharton and his colleagues at Shope Reno Wharton Architecture aren't interested in reproducing historical structures. Rather, they're committed to utilizing their vast body of knowledge to create fresh, original residences that have a distinct timeless quality.

Though every project is entirely unique, based on its site and its future residents, the architects always begin by surveying the neighborhood to get a sense of what, architecturally, has gone on before. They encourage clients to set aside any preconceptions of what their house should look like and, instead, focus on what they want their home to feel like and how it should function. From those intangible desires, the architects create extraordinary homes that respond to the locale, make a profound architectural statement, and enhance the quality of life for all who dwell within.

"I'm always thinking 100 years out. We have every reason to build homes of enduring quality."

—Bernard Wharton

SHOPE RENO WHARTON ARCHITECTURE

"Choosing local materials gives the architecture a certain level of authenticity, recalling the days when people simply made the best of the materials the site had to offer."

—Bernard Wharton

TOP & FACING PAGE: Two libraries, two patrons, one house. His space, defined by the dramatic oak-beam coffered ceiling, can be used as an office, quiet space for reading, or card game room for entertaining. On the opposite side of the entry court, her library is also a classically derived multipurpose space with an intimate ambience, but the manifestation is quite different. Deeply stained mahogany frames the barrel-vaulted ceiling for a formal elegance.

BOTTOM: Sloping sites have their fair share of challenges, but they offer the opportunity to create architecture that emerges naturally from the land. The Shingle-style home has a variety of terraces conducive to indoor-outdoor living; several French doors connect the indoor pool to nature; steps cascade from the lower terrace to the lawn. By working with the site rather than against it, we created a home that looks and feels like it was meant to be.

PREVIOUS PAGES LEFT: The home responds to modern-day needs while embodying all of the style and grace synonymous with the Georgian vernacular. Defined by arches, pilasters, and generous custom mouldings, the space reads as a wonderful series of galleries, rather than an overwhelming corridor. Appropriate to the period, the crispness of the white perfectly balances the warm herringbone-patterned oak floor with walnut border.

PREVIOUS PAGES RIGHT: It's important to consider the fabric of the neighborhood before weaving in a new building. The new structure doesn't need to precisely echo its surroundings but it certainly must take them into account. For a couple who wanted a vacation home that paid homage to the Shingle style, we designed a haven that embraces its incredible bluff setting much like an amphitheater and takes advantage of views to the sailboat-lined harbor.
Photographs by Durston Saylor

"A building should feel effortless as it weds itself with the ground."

—Bernard Wharton

ABOVE: Entry sequences deserve careful planning. While the front elevation offers the first visual impression of a home, the journey to the front door really sets up the whole architectural experience. Guests step out of the car and are immediately met by rhythms, paths, details, and materials that subtly pull them toward the home. A series of planes and experiences direct them to the front door. Libraries flank the front entrance of the home, which is clad in a special blend of stones. We didn't want the façade to look like a sea of grey or brown sameness, so we pulled fieldstones of different sizes and shapes from four different quarries to create a rich, organic, patchwork effect.

FACING PAGE: A room derives power from the proportions and scale, not the ornamentation. In the living room, you don't read each beam of the ceiling, you read the rhythm of them. We tied that experience into details throughout the room in the horizontality of the chair rail, fireplace mantel, and cornice work. To draw attention to the ground plane, we specified a soft white ceiling and light blue walls.

Photographs by Durston Saylor

"Green design is common sense. It's about magnifying the things we've been doing for thousands of years."

—Bernard Wharton

ABOVE: We designed the waterfront home expressly for casual, indoor-outdoor family gatherings. The living, dining, and kitchen areas are wide open and infused with plenty of natural light. Because the home has southern exposure, we designed deep overhangs to shade the expansive porch and to keep the indoor temperature down without sacrificing quality of light.

FACING PAGE: Upside-down houses are always a fun challenge. Dunes separate the site from the Atlantic, so we developed the floorplan with bedrooms on the lower level and spaces used mostly during the day on the upper level, for expansive views to the water.
Photographs by Durston Saylor

"Many architectural wonders of ancient civilizations are still standing—proof that there's no substitute for time-tested materials or tried-and-true construction methodologies."

—Bernard Wharton

ABOVE LEFT & RIGHT: With classical French and Georgian influences, the estate's full façade gently arcs to embrace the terraces and sizeable fountain. Overhangs and deep recesses create drama as shadows dance across the home throughout the day and even more so at night. The residence has a stately, formal character, making it ideal for elaborate galas and other social gatherings. Chimneys, beautiful in their vertical expression, punctuate the corners of the house. Enhancing the integration of architecture and site, the whole property is brilliantly landscaped.

FACING PAGE: Given a very tight urban site, we knew that frontloading the house—putting it at the front of the property, rather than right in the middle—was the best way to maximize space and keep the design from feeling like an infill project. With power derived from symmetry and density of detailing, the home is defined by classical elegance; it boldly engages the street and has an incredible backyard with plenty of privacy.
Photographs by Durston Saylor

Designing a house requires continual communication between the architect, the project team, and the future homeowner. Through hundreds of completed projects since its founding in 1989, Brewster Thornton Group Architects uses a gradually unfolding communication and design process, along with its impeccable relationship with industry professionals, to create an individual, beautiful, and satisfying dwelling.

From the first exciting vision through the completion of the residence, the architects guide the design in a direction that reflects both the homeowner and the location of the property. Brewster Thornton Group brings a wide range of possible solutions to the table and integrates each participant's response to better steer the project toward completion. Led by founder Mary Brewster, AIA, partner Barbara Thornton, AIA, and partner Nathaniel Ginsburg, AIA, the whole architectural team acts as a navigator for each family embarking on a new construction or renovation project.

Through understanding a family's day-to-day life and identifying images that speak to the family members, Brewster Thornton Group designs a home that complements the surroundings and resonates with the homeowners.

"A home's most important role is to pull a family closer together through the design's thoughtful functionality and delightful individuality."

—Mary Brewster

BREWSTER THORNTON GROUP ARCHITECTS, LLP

"The entryway of a house is like the cover of a book—it sets the stage and establishes an expectation about the rest of the house."

—Mary Brewster

TOP & BOTTOM: We created a soft boundary between the inside and outside with a glimpse of water from the front door to suggest a sense of outdoor living. From the entry stone that is carried through to the fireplace facing to a repetition of curves in the moulding profiles and china cabinet shapes, the exceptional details lead to harmony throughout the home.

FACING PAGE TOP & BOTTOM: Our challenge was to create a space that encompassed an open design and still responded to human scale. The foyer columns and trim bands at mid-height in the family room frame the space while the fireplace and consistent design details, such as the stair newel and fireplace brackets, anchor the rooms.

PREVIOUS PAGES: The homeowners wanted to preserve the traditional massing and feel of a seaside residence even though the house encompassed 5,000 square feet. We incorporated a simple, refined style with a steeply pitched roof and strong towers to evoke a sense of welcome and stability and to minimize a large façade. Porches and balconies open to the water on the rear.
Photographs by Warren Jagger Photography

"Instead of a collection of random architectural ideas, we choose a language of a few related elements and carry them throughout the project to bring balance and restfulness."

—Mary Brewster

ABOVE: The inspiration for the exterior came from the homeowner's love of classic Palm Beach architecture. We created a version that felt at home in New England through the use of limestone and granite siding with a slate roof and rough stone tower.
Photograph by Warren Jagger Photography

FACING PAGE: The couple, who had a grown family, desired elegant detail paired with a comfortable scale and maintenance-free materials. We accommodated the couple's request for an abundance of stone and used neo-classical elements to bind the design together. The end result is a gracious, inviting home that provides something new to notice upon each visit.
Top left photograph by Nat Rea Photography
Top right & bottom photographs by Warren Jagger Photography

"We love injecting emotion into a building. Each space can evoke a unique response through attention to scale, light, and texture."

—Mary Brewster

ABOVE: The family focused on the importance of natural light in the compact home, so we oriented the living spaces on the south side. The living room became a fusion of art and antique display with a comfortable ambience for a growing family.

RIGHT: We integrated a buffet for dual function—to accommodate the homeowners' art and pottery collection and to emphasize the connection between the dining and living rooms. The handmade tile countertop for the buffet transforms function into art.

FACING PAGE TOP: In the entry hall, the living room screen helps achieve an open feel, and the fir trim welcomes people throughout the house with the continuity of material.

FACING PAGE BOTTOM: The homeowners requested we create an Arts-and-Crafts bungalow to showcase their collection of Stickley furniture and period accessories. The front porch with timberwork and classic bungalow massing maintains the tradition of the house and neighborhood, while a low, sloping roof minimizes the presence from the street.
Photographs by Warren Jagger Photography

"Reusing an existing building provides an additional set of constraints that is both challenging and inspiring."

—Jai Singh Khalsa

LEFT & FACING PAGE: The Oxford House in Newton, Massachusetts, demonstrates the innovative reuse of an existing historic building. Originally an auditorium-style Christian Science church, the new 11 high-end housing units range in size from 1,200 to 3,000 square feet. To maintain the exterior, which was regulated by the local historic society, we worked the window pattern into the design and created special areas to utilize both the steeple and the front pediment. Inside, we created parking in the former recreation room in the basement and added two levels of housing and a mezzanine level.
Photographs by Kevin Burke

PREVIOUS PAGES: Among tall trees, we designed a simple, horizontal element to accommodate the homeowner's simple lifestyle while highlighting the natural verticality of the forest. We added abstract style and incorporated the owner's request for multiple fireplaces in order to provide natural heating. The large sliding windows on the projecting mass allow the homeowner to feel even more in tune with the surroundings.
Photographs by Nick Wheeler

LEFT: In one unit's library at The Oxford House, we had Brazilian carpenters create custom built-ins for the space to blend with the church's original plaster moulding detail, which we maintained throughout the building. A Lennox gas fireplace adds warmth to the room, while the high ceilings are grounded by the use of coffers.
Photograph by Kevin Burke

"A fresh, modern architectural style can be an exceptional way to show off fantastic artwork."

—Jai Singh Khalsa

LEFT & FACING PAGE: We drew inspiration for the renovation from the condominium's location on Commonwealth Avenue in Boston, where magnolia trees beautifully line the street. In merging two units into one 1,750-square-foot corner condo, we transformed the antiquated rooms with large mirrors, ornate handrails, and extra wood trim by opening up the main spaces and creating several more intimate spaces that intermingled with the kitchen and living areas. The owners had beautiful artwork, so we focused on clean lines to minimize the distractions.

Photographs by Dusan Radakovic

Bacco, Inc., page 63

Kirby Perkins Construction, page 93

the structure

chapter two

E.W. Tarca Construction, page 83

Y F I Custom Homes, page 113

The Classic Group, page 73

For more than 20 years the full-service general contracting firm Bacco, Inc. has built and renovated some of the most extraordinary homes found along the East Coast, primarily in Fairfield and Upper Westchester counties. Specializing in the high-end residential market, Bacco, Inc. has gained an outstanding reputation for its new custom home, renovation, and addition projects.

The firm's demanding clientele expect superior quality and service—and that is what Bacco, Inc. provides. The majority of contracts are derived from word-of-mouth referrals and repeat business. Indeed, Bacco, Inc. has had the privilege of building a custom dream home for a client, renovating it a few years later, and even later on building another residence for the same client. These types of relationships are not uncommon for Bacco, Inc. Of course, with consistently superior quality and craftsmanship delivered from a cadre of time-tested skilled carpenters, Bacco, Inc. is able to exceed expectations time and time again. Combining this resolute commitment to quality with talent and exceptional service has garnered the firm renown as a premier general contractor.

"Perfection is not too much to ask for."

—Kenneth Bacco

BACCO, INC.

ABOVE: The outdoor setting is pure elegance. It has two remarkable pool pavilions with eight sides of glass, motorized skylights, and interior glass partitions; the enchanting fountain and lily pond are set among hand-carved limestone shelves.

FACING PAGE TOP: Exquisite craftsmanship abounds throughout the corridor. Our artisan-caliber carpenters crafted remarkable interior details and trimwork from walnut and limestone.

FACING PAGE BOTTOM: Abundant natural light draws attention to the coffered ceilings and antique European limestone fireplace. Custom herringbone floors complement the antique mantel.

PREVIOUS PAGES LEFT: Homeowners step through the front door into supreme elegance; the winding, self-supporting staircase with hand-carved wood railing and custom metal balustrade exudes grace and sophistication.

PREVIOUS PAGES RIGHT: An outstanding example of Shingle-style architecture, the waterfront residence in Greenwich, Connecticut, won an Alice Washburn Award in 2007 and features a unique blend of traditional materials like wood, stone, and shingle on an extraordinary piece of property.
Photographs by Tim Lee

"A well-built home will age gracefully without losing its timeless character."

—Kenneth Bacco

ABOVE: Rustic charm is on full display at a French Country home in Connecticut; the stonework, natural materials, and integration into the landscape make the residence inviting.

FACING PAGE: The process of transforming a barn into a dream home led to incorporating the existing silo in a novel way: A beautiful wine cellar exists behind the stonework while a reading room above aligns with the window to provide an exterior connection.
Photographs by Tim Lee

ABOVE: In the light-filled living room of a waterfront home, antique chestnut floors, coffered ceilings, rich woodwork, and hand-painted tiles around the fireplace create the desired ambience.

FACING PAGE TOP: Delicately set atop a knoll with a beautiful driveway leading up to it, the house has a classic look enhanced by a stately slate roof and hand-chiseled stone veneer.

FACING PAGE BOTTOM: The stair tower rising between two floors displays superior craftsmanship in mahogany beams, staircases, and everywhere else; the luxurious wine room is made of cherry with African slate on the floor.
Photographs by Tim Lee

"Superior craftsmanship is not a single act but an everyday approach to excellence."

—Kenneth Bacco

ABOVE: The front façade is comprised of beautiful Belgian block, handsome corbels, and magnificent gable forms; tight quarters and the goal of preserving a mature tree in back presented unique challenges, which we successfully overcame.

FACING PAGE: A waterfront home of impeccable refinement features a seamless progression through the interior spaces, which feature quarter-sawn herringbone floors with walnut inlay, luxurious wainscoting, and grand columns.
Photographs by Tim Lee

Kyle Barnard and Philip Bates have mastered time travel—so to speak. The Massachusetts team spent years fine-tuning the tricky art of historical home building and restoration, a trade that both preserves the past and gives residents a chance to transport back in time.

The Classic Group began in 1986 under the premise that people who love traditional architecture should be able to enjoy it with all the comforts of modernity. Pulling in history, geography, culture, and ingenuity, Philip and Kyle realize the company's founding goals, collaborating with a selected team for each project. The core team consists of a project manager, an architect—either in-house or client selected—and the homeowners. Whether it be an interior restoration or new construction, The Classic Group recreates a project's time period in the most extraordinary detail and precision. With homes spanning the late 1700s into the early 20th century, The Classic Group helps Georgian, American Colonial, and Greek Revival come to life.

"Good ideas should always prevail. The benefit of a collaborative approach is that team members constantly challenge one another, allowing only the best designs to remain."

—Philip Bates

THE CLASSIC GROUP

ABOVE & FACING PAGE: When homeowners wanted a one-story addition to their 1904 residence, we discovered significant insect damage. Because so many of our projects have seen a century of weathering, our discovery was not uncommon. Cases like this give us a chance to invest in the home's longevity. In keeping with a traditional standard of quality, we used rot-resistant wood species for all the exterior trim, avoiding pine and other materials that are susceptible to decay from exposure to the elements.
Photographs by Sam Gray

PREVIOUS PAGES LEFT: A Georgian Revival from the 1930s captures popular patterns of the time: elliptical arches. Featured on the exterior of the home as well, the elliptical arches define the renovated hallway and mahogany service space; the dining room and pantry lie to each side.
Photograph by John Horner

PREVIOUS PAGES RIGHT: Bostonians of the past built their summer homes outside of the city as an escape from the often-oppressive heat. As a result, towns like Newton and Brookline boast traditional luxury homes from long ago. In order to maintain the integrity of these classic homes during reconstruction, we add modern amenities just as they might have appeared in the home's original era. A Georgian Revival from 1903 exhibits this, integrating radiant heat into the flooring while encapsulating the style of an 18th-century sitting room. The solarium lies just beyond.
Photograph by Eric Roth

"It's important to save architecture from the past. We don't want to replace elements with historical significance when refurbishment is an option."

—Kyle Barnard

ABOVE LEFT: Bathrooms are a common room to add while renovating a historic home—and possibly the most personal. Whether a suite for the homeowners or a powder room for guests, bathrooms demand a great deal of attention during the design and build phases. An ornate black and white master bath includes an opaque glass window, relocated from the sun porch, and connects to a dressing room for extended private space.
Photograph by Eric Roth

ABOVE RIGHT: We carefully maintained the home's architectural vocabulary within the powder room. Leaded glass and elliptical patterns reoccur throughout the house, appearing in fanlights, case openings, French door designs, and areas of the kitchen. Primarily meant for guests, the intimate white-washed powder room quickly charms anyone who enters.
Photograph by John Horner

FACING PAGE: American chestnut brings rustic warmth to a mudroom—the first room to welcome residents as they pass through the basement-level entry. The space captures an Old World charm by using reclaimed materials: the flooring is comprised of French roof tiles while the chestnut was salvaged locally.
Photograph by Eric Roth

"Working with historical homes is the best way to develop a strong level of anticipation, the ability to see what's ahead."

—Kyle Barnard

TOP: Nothing highlights a home's outdated technology like the kitchen, which is why so many have to be built anew. Here we created an eat-in area, full fireplace, and highly functional cooking spaces for a full addition.
Photograph by Eric Roth

BOTTOM: The character of a 1930s Eleanor Raymond home needs to be carefully observed during a restoration. We brought in light and expanded the space, turning a galley kitchen into a full, more accessible kitchen. Opening the flow of travel through the home, the new design includes an informal seating area at the island plus a dedicated area for food preparation. The ceiling beam marks our movement of the wall, allowing residents to update the room while appreciating the original design.
Photograph by Eric Roth

FACING PAGE: A historic Boston building is gutted down to the concrete in order to completely redesign the interior. The family-oriented residents wanted a classic Boston Brahmin retreat, resulting in immense detail throughout the home—particularly in the central kitchen.
Photograph by Sam Gray

"Constantly assessing the house—inspecting roofs, windows, every detail—ensures the home's character will remain."

—Philip Bates

ABOVE: Indoor pools are one of the most challenging structures to design and build. With the combination of cold New England winters, indoor humidity of the pool house, and the abundance of windows, the risks for condensation and moisture problems are high. The building must be completely airtight, well insulated, and include a carefully engineered airflow system. Access to this freestanding pool house comes via an 80-foot tunnel from the main house that also serves as an art gallery. Family and guests use his-and-hers changing rooms in the basement before ascending stairs to the 25-meter pool, whirlpool, two showers, and caterer's kitchen. With a well-illuminated, intersecting barrel-vaulted ceiling and hand-painted murals, this structure transforms into a magnificent entertaining space. The pool gets year-round use by the whole family as well as serves as a regular venue for entertaining friends and hosting charity events.
Photograph courtesy of The Classic Group

FACING PAGE LEFT: Located just outside of Boston, a Greek Revival-inspired guest house sits adjacent to the main house, showing off the strong lines of a classic temple. Even though the project is all new construction, we designed the wood columns and used Colorado sandstone to complement the Georgian style of the primary house. Spearheaded by the homeowner, the project began with a desire to re-incorporate land that once existed as a single piece of property. Managing to capture the most important parcels, the homeowner has restored the estate's impressive scale and established the perfect combination of formality and outdoor living—just as the original estate once had.
Photograph by Sam Gray

FACING PAGE RIGHT: The size of a house should not affect its ability to make a statement, particularly when it's a classical residence from the Georgian era. With the original door and transom in place, the entryway announces the formality of the home. Its period detail and regimented structure adds to a strong character.
Photograph courtesy of The Classic Group

A premier custom builder, E.W. Tarca Construction has an architecturally diverse portfolio. Having grown his business largely on referrals, Ed Tarca is responsible for hundreds of new homes and thoughtful renovations throughout Massachusetts.

Ed built the company on principles of honesty and integrity. Every craftsman who works on a project is a professional at his craft and in his demeanor. With each project, the E.W. Tarca team considers how homeowners live, work, relax, and entertain. Utilizing innovative techniques, superb craftsmanship, and the highest quality materials, they keep present and future wants and needs in mind as they build. And most importantly, the construction process is managed with transparency, accountability, and respect for the homeowner's schedule and budget.

One of the company's secrets to success is its proprietary high-tech millwork shop, which enables complete control over the aesthetic and quality of the woodwork as well as the associated cost and delivery of materials. Owners are invited to visit the shop as key elements of their home are fabricated. And because of E.W. Tarca's extensive network of specialty craftsmen and technology integrators, the company can bring to fruition even the most complex and challenging projects.

"Each site has limitless possibilities. The builder's job is to help homeowners find the possibilities that most closely match their dreams and then bring those dreams to life."

—Ed Tarca

E.W. TARCA CONSTRUCTION

"Painstakingly planning and implementing the technical details within a home's walls and under the landscape allows greater flexibility to make changes or add capability down the road. It's definitely energy well spent."

—Ed Tarca

ABOVE: Because of the home's proximity to the ocean, we used fiberglass siding and polyvinyl chloride trim with custom mouldings to achieve a low-maintenance, Cape Cod style.
Photograph courtesy of John Dvorsack

FACING PAGE: We incorporated classic New England elements—wood shingles, stone veneer, and wrought iron—with unique details, such as a circular staircase in the tower and design-rich windows, to create a house that feels like it's miles from the city when it's minutes from the interstate.
Photograph by Richard Mandelkorn

PREVIOUS PAGES: By using a variety of fine building materials, including stone veneer and clapboard siding, slate on the roof, custom-cut limestone accents, and heavy fir beams in the walkway, we enabled the 15,000-square-foot home's beautiful detailing to take center stage. The materials palette magic begins in our design center, which has hundreds of samples of woods, mouldings, cabinet doors, flooring, granite, and hardware, among other elements. Being able to see and touch a variety of materials really helps to simplify the selection process.
Photograph by Eric Roth

"There is innate joy in watching a project evolve from a vision or photograph to a finished residence, a place where a family can find respite and love."

—Ed Tarca

LEFT: The columns and cabinetry we crafted in our mill make the hallway an inviting space. The circular staircase at the end of the hall rises from the lower level up to the master suite for a beautiful transition between the living spaces.
Photograph by Alex Beatty

FACING PAGE: The captain's quarters look of the living area, with its arched maple beadboard ceiling, maple doors, and ocean mural, satisfies the homeowners' love of all things nautical.
Photograph courtesy of John Dvorsack

"The real fun is in the details."

—Ed Tarca

ABOVE: We hand carved the ventilation hood and the cherry cabinets to give the kitchen a life of its own.
Photograph by Eric Roth

RIGHT: We transformed a built-in storage cabinet and wet bar into the kitchen's focal point with decorative painting, glazing, and the addition of mirrors—an unexpected touch of sophistication.
Photograph by Michael J. Lee

FACING PAGE TOP: Because the conservatory needed to blend seamlessly with the existing Federal-style home, we used nearly 800 pieces of cast stone to create a harmonious, formal look.
Photograph courtesy of Alex Beatty

FACING PAGE BOTTOM: We designed the indoor lap pool and hot tub to mimic a Roman spa with a barrel ceiling and stone columns to support the arches. Venetian plaster walls and Jerusalem limestone flooring and pool copings give the space a finished look.
Photograph courtesy of John Ferrarone

"Leaving no stone unturned in the planning stages leads to a truly great home and happy owners."

—Ed Tarca

ABOVE LEFT: We hand scraped and glazed fir beams to impart depth and a weathered outdoor look for the ceiling. The rounded curves of the custom bed and built-in dresser, porthole window, and steel cable railing on the outside deck evoke images of the bow of a boat.
Photograph courtesy of John Dvorsack

ABOVE RIGHT: We crafted the cherry vanity with unending detail to complement the arched ceiling, travertine floors, and luxurious shower.
Photograph by Eric Roth

FACING PAGE: The billiard room of a 9,000-square-foot home offered high ceilings, so we added nonstructural beams of hand-rubbed mahogany and used Venetian plaster on the walls to enhance the rich patina of the wood.
Photograph courtesy of John Ferrarone

When Jerry Kirby has a vision, he dreams big. So once he decided to become a professional bowman, he took every possible opportunity that came his way. With his role in sailing, Jerry has the privilege of meeting the inherently interesting people that the sport draws. He has the chance to meet property owners all over the Northeast and create long-lasting friendships.

Much of Jerry's Kirby Perkins Construction team is comprised of top-notch men with a background in boat building. He elaborates that "nautical engineering provides almost no room for error, giving each craftsman an amazing eye for detail."

Currently, Jerry is competing in the Volvo Ocean Race on board *Il Mostro*, team Puma. The race takes the men to ports such as Singapore, Galway, and Rio de Janeiro. With an itinerary like this, Jerry doesn't have to prove that he loves adventure—he lives it. People are drawn to Jerry's infectious, positive spirit. That same spirit shows up in his work on land, building and restoring homes in some of New England's most dynamic locations.

"We feel connected to a different generation of craftsmen."

—Jerry Kirby

KIRBY PERKINS CONSTRUCTION

RIGHT: I started Kirby Construction in 1980, splitting my time between building boats, sailboat racing, and the construction business. Joining with longtime friend and brother-in-law Tom Perkins, we formed Kirby Perkins Construction in 1995. Our team includes painters, carpenters, millworkers, roofers, welders, and draftsmen who put their energy behind restoration projects like Doris Duke's Rough Point. The mansion shows off the same skill that appears in Kirby Perkins' historic preservation projects across Newport including Peabody & Stearns' Vanderbilt Mansion, Whitney Warren's Newport Country Club, McKim, Mead and White's Isaac Bell House, and George Mason Jr.'s Rock Cliff to name a few.

PREVIOUS PAGES: For a family who loves to sail, we constructed a nautical-themed home on waterfront property in Newport. A sail loft above the garage plus teak and holly flooring reflect the owners' lifestyle and interests. The scope of the project was designed to reduce each structure's mass while still accommodating large numbers of guests. Two outbuildings sit nearby, a guest cottage, woodworking shop with radiant heating, garage, and potting shed make up the compound.

Photographs by Larry Lambrecht

"A triangle of elements drives every project: scope, quality, and cost. The importance of each must be weighed before plans can proceed."

—Tom Perkins

ABOVE & FACING PAGE: Constructing from the ground up, we built a coastal contemporary home on piers and included breakaway panels due to the site's location in a high-velocity flood zone. The severe climate of Narragansett Bay in Portsmouth, Rhode Island, presents a challenge for any structure; we knew it had to hold up during hurricanes and floods. No aesthetic value was sacrificed—the home is stunning. The extensive use of steel framing helped to achieve this look, giving the home a complex roof and expansive ceilings. Modern materials used in our projects enable our team to improve durability without compromising design.
Photographs by Eric Roth

"New England's most accomplished architects are a great resource for staying ahead of the evolving technology of building construction."

—Tom Perkins

ABOVE & FACING PAGE: A private residence in Middletown, Rhode Island, shows off a Roman slate roof that gives the home an Old World feel. Exposed fir beams with mortised hand-forged black iron hangers maintain the same sentiment for the interior.
Photographs by Warren Jagger

"When highly skilled architects and builders collaborate, the dynamics are apparent in the home's aesthetic."

—Tyler Finkle

RIGHT & FACING PAGE: Although historic preservation and restoration make up a great deal of our projects, custom homes remain as a sizable portion of our business. A Little Compton, Rhode Island, residence set in a rural environment with breathtaking scenery was value engineered by our site supervisor virtually on CAD software prior to construction. This process enables for greater efficiencies throughout the many logistical aspects of the building process.

Photographs by Warren Jagger

Since building his first house in 1978, Marc Kaplan knew what he wanted to do. With a civil engineering degree under his belt, Marc began homebuilding in the Boston area, quickly making a name for himself. Through decades of work and dedication, he's not only gained an impressive portfolio, but a tremendous understanding of the industry—proven by Sanford Custom Builders.

In a competitive market filled with endless options, what makes Sanford Custom Builders stand out from the rest? As principal, Marc knows that his attention to each project is crucial to its success, which is exactly why he never takes on more than he can manage. Doling out or divvying up the hard work never happens, allowing Marc to adhere to his standards and maintain a closer relationship with his crew and collaborators. Insisting that teamwork is everything, Marc surrounds himself with highly professional, qualified people to get the job done. The most remarkable homes come from a solid team with four critical members: the builder, architect, interior designer, and landscape architect. Once that bond is established and communication is clear, the home is a sure-fire success.

"Natural elements are always a sound investment. Stone, wood, and marble have a timeless appeal."

—Marc Kaplan

SANFORD CUSTOM BUILDERS

RIGHT: One of the most complicated projects in homebuilding is the indoor pool. The challenges are many; humidity and moisture control take a great deal of problem solving in the Massachusetts climate. But the end results are well worth it, giving residents a year-round space for leisure and recreation.

PREVIOUS PAGES: Our work has to fit the personality of the family. For a traditional Georgian home, we gave the rear exterior a fun, whimsical feel where the family could relax. Integrating brick and copper along with a calming landscape design helped us achieve that mood. And to create an air of formality and elegance in a classic foyer, we placed marble floors with custom borders and inlays beneath a floating, curved staircase—perfect for the residents.

Photographs by Sam Gray

"Put together a solid team before building a home; the team members' ability to function well together will make all the difference."

—Marc Kaplan

ABOVE LEFT & RIGHT: Every home incorporates elements that are singular to the owners. We used a fireplace inspired by a lodge in Kenya that looked stunning against a limestone floor and iron balustrades with wood posts. And for residents who wanted jaws to drop as guests entered the dining room, we built a barrel-vaulted ceiling; the strong curves of the design never fail to impress.

Left photograph by Sam Gray
Right photograph by Alex Beatty

FACING PAGE: Stone and wood offer a rustic quality that works well in almost any capacity. When used for a screened-in porch, the materials present a nostalgic feel, reminiscent of summers spent in the woods of Maine; when used on an exterior, they add classic appeal and a welcoming façade. The exotic species have a similar effect—we built a kitchen with Tasmanian myrtle floors and solid bubinga tree countertops.

Photographs by Sam Gray

LEFT: A Shingle-style home in the Boston area emphasizes our highly detailed work. A complicated chimney design—with chimney pots—and wood roof reveal the craftsmanship of our team.

Photograph by Kallan MacLeod

custom homebuilding 109

> "For a custom home, nothing is off limits."
>
> —Marc Kaplan

ABOVE: Easily mistaken for a hunting lodge, a Massachusetts home highlights our extensive stone work—strong yet refined. To add to the naturalistic environment, we built a soothing waterfall feature and koi pond that lets the homeowners observe and interact with nature.

Photograph by Sam Gray

FACING PAGE: Wood is a popular material in homes; but it takes keen design to show off its full potential. We collaborated with an architect who uses meticulous woodwork in a variety of ways—all equally stunning. From reclaimed walnut and pine floors to a complex elliptical staircase, the use of wood gives classic beauty to each room.

Photographs by Kallan MacLeod

A lively weekend dinner in a New England coastal home is a common sight. But when the guest is the homebuilder from five years ago, the scene becomes a bit more unusual. Yet this is exactly the kind of relationship that Glenn Farrell and his team at YFI Custom Homes maintain with the homeowners—one of friendship and communication amidst a close-knit community.

Glenn got his start in real estate as a CPA advising on real estate projects, but began to desire more tangible results from his work. Given his longstanding love and knowledge of woodworking that he gleaned from carpentry work during college, Glenn moved first toward building spec homes and then to custom homes.

Through partnerships with only the best architects and subcontractors, Glenn has used his excellent organizational skills to create a team that seamlessly builds homes. Glenn and his team have become experts in beautiful, sustainable construction, which is evident from his first project more than 20 years ago with a closed-loop geothermal heat pump to his recent involvement in Builder20, a group of builders who share ideas and news about new products and techniques.

"One of the thrills in homebuilding comes when an owner who has waited many years finally sees his dream home come to life."

—Glenn Farrell

Y F I CUSTOM HOMES

"A satisfaction exists in homebuilding from leaving a legacy that will endure through many generations."

—Glenn Farrell

ABOVE & FACING PAGE: We wanted to ensure a residence overlooking a lighthouse was both beautiful and able to withstand hurricane-force winds and rising water. With input from TMS Architects, we used a steel frame for the home and built an 18-foot retaining wall along the water's edge, which we backfilled to create a yard. We also blasted down 30 feet to create a wine cellar, then dug a tunnel out to the water's edge, at which point watertight doors, when open, frame the view of the lighthouse.
Photographs by Karosis Photographic

PREVIOUS PAGES: In our woodworking shop, we crafted a custom walnut ceiling, fireplace surround, and an arched entryway, and then cut reclaimed chestnut beams from an old mill into beautiful flooring for installation into the home. For a world-traveling consultant, we built a two-story library complete with a ladder and hidden compartments in the mahogany bookcases to blend with the African sapele floor.
Left photograph by Joseph St. Pierre Photography
Right photograph by Karosis Photographic

"Unexpected challenges, such as regional floods during construction, are not what make or break a project. It's the attitude and process of regrouping that impacts the work."

—Glenn Farrell

ABOVE: The first challenge was the lot restrictions that limited the floorplan to the existing footprint, and second with the nearby road being washed out for two weeks during construction. To accommodate the footprint issue, we stripped the existing home to a shell and rebuilt it utilizing every inch of space through techniques like custom cabinets to hold electronics and double as seating. We also built a waterproof dike at the back of the house to prevent any flooding in the future.

FACING PAGE: For a renovation and addition on a historical sea captain's home, we first modernized the mechanical systems and updated the bathrooms, then crafted a bright kitchen at the back of the home with numerous windows to take advantage of the gorgeous views. The homeowners were pleasantly surprised, especially since they were living in Paris at the time and only visited the house a few times during construction.
Photographs by Joseph St. Pierre Photography

Jozef Custom Ironworks, Inc., page 155

Cara-Donna Copper and Slate Co., page 129

elements of structure

chapter three

Crown Point Cabinetry, page 121

Blazing Design, page 139

South Shore Millwork, page 159

Claremont, New Hampshire

"People are moving toward building a smaller footprint but focusing more on the quality and details in the home."

—Brian Stowell

ABOVE & FACING PAGE: To achieve the distinctive color the homeowners desired, we created a custom-blended yellow for the beaded inset maple cabinetry. The island and pass-through cabinets, which were crafted out of reclaimed antique heart pine from Carlisle Wide Plank Floors, provide a warm counterpoint in Burnt Umber stain. The inclusion of stacked moulding gives the room height and a touch of formality while the appliance panels concealing the refrigerator, wine cooler, and dishwasher provide a cohesive feel.
Photographs by Crown Point Cabinetry

"The best years of my life have been spent learning woodworking and cabinetry from my dad and being part of the family business."

—Brian Stowell

ABOVE & FACING PAGE: A Victorian style permeates the sophisticated kitchen, from the beaded inset maple cabinetry, to the paneled columns of the island, to the multipaned glass doors. The two-part, built-up crown moulding and the beautiful hood mantel with carved corbels and spice pullouts on the sides exude elegance. Our Antique White Classic Paint provides a sense of poise across the extensive details and a built-in hutch painted in Seabrook Green adds vintage-style charm. We continued the Victorian appeal on the hutch and desk with details in the valance, toekick, and pigeonhole drawers. The adjacent mahogany wet bar features our Amherst doors, which are crafted with raised applied moulding for a rich, luxurious allure.

Photographs by Crown Point Cabinetry

"Tools and technology for cabinetmaking have evolved so dramatically, allowing for more cost-effective customization and design flexibility."

—Brian Stowell

TOP: A Vermont home called for a blush of urban style coupled with comfortable country living. We mixed a custom color to complement the beautiful handmade tile and emphasized the sleek design with our flat-paneled Newport door. The island, a study in contrast with cherry hardwood and Chestnut stain, includes drawer storage for spices, integral hand-turned legs, and full-height doors for easy access.

BOTTOM: In a Boston brownstone, the uniquely configured cabinetry provides a well-executed workflow in a compact space while maintaining the important open area between the kitchen and adjoining rooms. Furthermore, the owner wanted to accent her own artwork with individual flair, so the cabinets were delivered primed and ready to incorporate her personal signature.

FACING PAGE: In a California home, we merged specialized functionality with an aesthetic quality. To satisfy worries about losing dishes and china in a lesser earthquake, as the homeowners had previously endured, we installed hidden rods to keep the cabinet doors closed. The maple cabinets were designed with a vintage look by using Barnstead doors, a milk-painted finish, and flush toekick runs up to the sink.

Photographs by Crown Point Cabinetry

"We feel like the elves in Santa's workshop, handcrafting cabinetry to clients' specifications and making wishes come true."

—Brian Stowell

ABOVE: I desired a Greek Revival feel in my own kitchen using columns, curved accents, and pediment tops. We then paired a custom-blended blue-green paint with a custom soft yellow for visual interest. Reclaimed chestnut from a 200-year-old barn in Virginia proved to be an extraordinary source out of which to construct the island and barstools.

FACING PAGE TOP: As featured in the 2005 *Country Living* Home of the Year, a light blue vanity turned an ordinary space into a work of art. The graceful arch spanning the width of the piece, the central drawer on the countertop, and the wispy fabric all add special touches that are charming and functional.

FACING PAGE BOTTOM: The vanity in the lakefront home features a dual bank of drawers, customized to fit around the plumbing, flanking a handsome set-back center element. Abutting the vanity, the wainscot panels on the tub are designed to be removable for easy access. A Victorian toekick treatment, Providence door style, and Steeple White Classic Paint maintain the cottage feel found in the rest of the home.

Photographs by Crown Point Cabinetry

Cara-Donna Copper and Slate Co.

Norwell, Massachusetts

"In addition to the beautiful aesthetic, copper and slate roofing offer exceptional benefits. These lifetime materials resist fire and corrosion, are incredibly strong, and offer environmental benefits as well."

—Bill Cara-Donna

ABOVE: On a project with Pearson Renovation, I hand-formed Revere FreedomGray™ copper on the cupola roof and finial. The naturally weathering grey tones complement the half-inch-thick North Country black slate on the utility shed roof.

FACING PAGE: My love of historical houses was increased by a turret addition on a house that was built by G.F. Rhode Construction and featured on PBS' "This Old House." As the standing seam copper weathers, it will change shades and further complement the weathering wood roof and siding to beautifully blend details of an older home with more contemporary lines of a newer home.
Photographs by William Cara-Donna

"The ancient art of laying slate and working by hand with copper is inspiring and brings out a sense of pride by doing things the old-fashioned way."

—Bill Cara-Donna

LEFT: During G.F. Rhode Construction's project in Chestnut Hill, Massachusetts, I cut each copper panel to fit the different-sized roof segments and hand-formed the standing seams to fit the curvature of the bell shape.

FACING PAGE TOP: To create variety and interest on a roof, I used Vermont slate in random sizes and four colors. The bell-shaped tower, topped by a custom finial, required me to hand-fit each copper panel and then use a hand-formed cap to cover each seam.

FACING PAGE BOTTOM: Each project provides unique challenges, especially with curving roofs. The copper cupola called for hand-forming as usual, and the slate had to be carefully applied to follow the curving flow of the eyebrow roof.
Photographs by William Cara-Donna

"Although the style of a house should be considered when choosing roofing, both copper and slate are versatile materials that can accommodate all types of homes, from contemporary to traditional to historic."

—Bill Cara-Donna

ABOVE: The historical style of the Pearson Renovations project called for half-inch black slate, built-in gutters with copper-clad chimney caps, flat roofs of soldered flat-seam copper, and decorative leaderheads at the top of each downspout. Because of the surrounding wetlands, we used a tin/zinc alloy-coated copper instead of the traditional copper and lead flashings.

FACING PAGE TOP: Because of the Newport Housewrights project's proximity to the ocean, I incorporated flashing details into the grey-black slate roof to account for wind-driven rains from the Atlantic storms. To the copper turrets that are finished with standing seam caps, I also added custom finials that function as lightning rods.

FACING PAGE BOTTOM: The unique roof design on the Newport Housewrights home curves not only from right to left, but also from the wall to the gutter edge. I laid out each panel in a trapezoidal pattern to allow for the fantail appearance of the roof. To accommodate the curves, I made a special tool to form the seams without damaging the copper panels.
Photographs by William Cara-Donna

"Technology doesn't have to be invasive to be state of the art."

—Jeff Haggar

ABOVE: We worked with the designer to seamlessly integrate home entertainment into the homeowners' décor and lifestyle. To the left of the fireplace, speakers blend into the home theater environment, while a center channel speaker sits inconspicuously on the mantel. All wires and components are carefully concealed to maintain the aesthetic appeal of the space.
Photograph courtesy of Audio Concepts

FACING PAGE: Collaborating with other design professionals always creates better results. For a Boston apartment, we worked with Karen Gilman of Finelines to incorporate her automated shades into the home control system for energy efficiency, privacy, and convenience. A cleverly concealed surround sound system complemented with a Lutron lighting control system allows the resident to set the mood of the space with the push of a button.
Photograph by Stephen SetteDucati

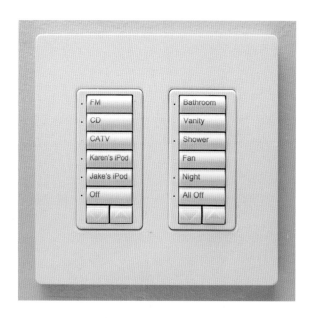

ABOVE: A Wellesley home's welcoming family room integrates energy efficiency, entertainment, and technology. Designed by Finelines, the window treatments offer a green aspect to the design. Motorized shading reduces energy bills while protecting upholstery, carpets, and floors from the harmful effects of harsh sunlight. When leaving the home, the owner simply pushes the "Away" button, which lowers the shades and turns off the lights, music, and television throughout the home. Always sensitive to the design elements in a project, we worked diligently with Michael Humphries Woodworking to design a cabinet that would accommodate the latest in technology without disrupting the aesthetic design scheme for the room. The cabinet features acoustically transparent panels that allow for speaker sound flow, and the center entertainment cabinet hides a speaker coupled with a subwoofer. All of these components work together for a clean, uncluttered effect. Collaboration is the only way to effectively incorporate all of a project's design and technology elements.
Photograph by Stephen SetteDucati

FACING PAGE TOP: Walls cluttered with light switches and dimmers are a designer's nightmare, so they are always thrilled when we show them solutions that control all of the home's lighting and home entertainment systems from a custom engraved, wall-mounted keypad. Our clients can maintain a consistent design aesthetic and enjoy the convenience and flexibility of activating preset lighting and entertainment scenes from a keypad mounted on the wall, by the bed, or in the car.
Photograph by Jeff Haggar

FACING PAGE MIDDLE: Surveillance cameras located throughout the property allow residents to monitor their homes efficiently and conveniently. We worked closely with the homeowners to create a security solution that protects their home when they're away with preset programming that replays their home lighting patterns over the last two weeks.
Photograph by .Jeff Haggar

FACING PAGE BOTTOM: Customization is the cornerstone of any successful design, and the audio system in a North End of Boston apartment is no exception. Created for a custom mantel, the system includes a custom speaker camouflaged in the middle of the mantel below a recessed television. All electronics are hidden around the corner for a clean, seamless look.
Photograph by Jeff Haggar

BLAZING DESIGN

"A fire evokes something primal, even therapeutic, unlike any other source of warmth."

—Michael Van Buren

ABOVE: We work in harmony with the fire feature's environment. The firepit was designed to sit at ground level so as not to obstruct the view of the mountains and to create a warm spot to dry off in the cool air. We also added a custom-spun copper dome to cover the firepit when not in use.

FACING PAGE: Working collaboratively with the architect and designer, as is our tradition, we designed a contemporary fireplace for a Vermont dining deck. We used a classic Rumford firebox design, which dates back to the 1700s, to radiate as much heat as possible back into the space. The stainless steel burner with simulated river stones, bluestone hearth and top, native fieldstone surround, and copper cap all combine to create a complementary mix of old and new.
Photographs by Susan Teare

"The warmth of a fire's glow provides a familiar comfort."

—Michael Van Buren

ABOVE: We raised the granite hearth for the fireplace to provide wood storage underneath and allow the heat to radiate directly out into the dining porch.

RIGHT: Designed with the landscape architect, four copper bowls were placed along an arced stone wall. Each bowl is four feet in diameter and will patina nicely over time.

FACING PAGE TOP: For thermal efficiency, the fireplace and chimney were designed and installed within the building's thermal envelope. Custom-fabricated doors and doorframe provide outside makeup air, minimizing the conditioned air used, increasing efficiency, and ensuring the smoke won't spill into the house.

FACING PAGE BOTTOM: An arch over the hearth adds strength and stability to the ageless beauty of the fieldstone fireplace. Modern features provide functionality behind the scenes, such as a gas log set with a chimney fan controlled to create a draft before gas is allowed to flow.
Photographs by Susan Teare

CUMAR, INC.

"Old World tradition and classic craftsmanship come through in our work. We've brought Verona, Italy, to New England."

—Carlotta Cubi

ABOVE & FACING PAGE : Elegant and classic, a custom bathroom captures the taste of the homeowners with sleek white Calcutta marble. Cutting the slabs of marble, in this case, was crucial to the room's appearance. We carefully bookmatched the entire design, ensuring that all of the pattern's veins match perfectly. In addition to the eye-catching, claw-foot tub, a large double shower, crown moulding, and beautiful stone baseboards make the space unforgettable. Our latest technology gives us the ability to cut and fabricate materials with the greatest of detail. We have two CNC machines that use computer generated programming to cut and finish any project imaginable. Our technology allows us to deliver the highest quality work in the healthiest environment possible, from sophisticated polishing equipment and pressurized water-jet cutting machine to the use of an advanced water treatment system.
Photographs courtesy of Cumar, Inc.

"A wide selection of stone—marble, granite, limestone, slate, travertine—is critical to creating the perfect look."

—Angelo Ivo Cubi

ABOVE: When clients came to us with tile they had chosen, we picked out statuario to match. Placed amongst a double vanity and delicate accessories, the marble is a stunning, rich white material that gives the room depth.

FACING PAGE TOP & BOTTOM: Costa Esmeralda granite, built up to present a thick edge, gives a striking color to kitchens. We travel around the world to spot the highest quality stone; Brazil, Italy, India, and Madagascar locations provide some of the finest quarries to gather selections.

FACING PAGE MIDDLE: A standard one-and-a-quarter inch, ogee edge worked perfectly in a custom home. By doing the simplest designs beautifully and the most complicated with the greatest care, our reputation has grown and established us as a leading force in the Boston region, whether for homes, hotels, or commercial buildings. Cabinet design by Martha Bovelli. *Photographs courtesy of Cumar, Inc.*

DeAngelis Iron Work, Inc.

South Easton, Massachusetts

"The process of restoring historical ironwork affords the opportunity to better understand the trade's history."

—Chris Connelly

ABOVE: Our work ranges from historically accurate restorations, like the fencing and gates surrounding Harvard Yard at Harvard University, to custom, ornamental designs in the residential and commercial marketplaces. We typically work with iron—both cast and wrought—stainless steel, bronze, and nickel silver media. For an oceanfront residence, we incorporated a rolling, horizontal wave pattern into the rail design. We installed custom cast bronze seashells at the crest of each wave in order to add a one-of-a-kind detail that the homeowner would enjoy.
Photograph by Chris Connelly

FACING PAGE: We worked with Sanford Homes of Wellesley to create iron and wood railings in a Massachusetts home. The substantial scrollwork within the iron panels was 100-percent hand forged—complete with tapered and "fishtailed" termini. Special care was taken to ensure that the openings in the rail were sized to be compliant with local building codes.
Photograph by Sam Gray

"Restoration work teaches us a great deal about the value of producing high-quality products in today's built environment."

—Chris Connelly

ABOVE LEFT & RIGHT: Our work is prominently featured in the main entry foyer of a beautiful home set in an upscale suburb of Boston. The railing is fabricated entirely of nickel silver material—a relatively new and exciting alloy related to the bronze family. Interlocking ovals were painstakingly formed and joined together to create the smooth and seemingly effortless flow that the homeowners desired. All connections are invisible and the rail features a uniform grained finish.
Photographs by Adam Rigoli

FACING PAGE: The new owner of a penthouse overlooking Boston Harbor sent us a photograph featuring a rail design that had literally been torn out of a home magazine. We specified the appropriate component sizes, attachment details, and finishing information required to replicate the railing on a stairway that featured very complex geometry. Every scroll is custom turned and every connection exemplifies the highest level of quality—which has long been our hallmark.
Photographs by Mark Flannery

" Custom parquet is a versatile component of interior design that helps to complete any décor, from classic to modern. "

—Alexandre Minton

ABOVE LEFT: To avoid a "bowling alley" effect, the oak herringbone pattern is good for the hallway, and introducing mahogany blocks emulates the idea of a border. I designed and cut parquet specifically for the area.

ABOVE RIGHT: Inlaid blocks of mahogany and ash within the squares give this classical parquet pattern a modern twist.

FACING PAGE: A timeless antique pattern found in European palaces and framed by a classical border adds life to the living room and unifies architectural and interior design elements. Artistically designed parquet complements furniture, making it appear more elegant and luxurious.
Photographs by Andre Aloshine, Aloshine Imagery

"Nothing defines custom more than beautifully designed parquet floors."

—Alexandre Minton

TOP & BOTTOM: Custom copper inlaid into an oak box continues a pattern used on the space's wall coverings and window treatments. The pattern is also a component of the inlaid medallion on the floor at the entrance foyer. Light coming through the window plays with the grain of the wood, shooting off the boards, highlighting the patterns, and yielding amazing variations of appeal that differ throughout the day.

FACING PAGE: I used a classical herringbone pattern of mahogany to complement an exposed brick chimney—a dominant design element—in a different part of the kitchen. The floor's imitation brick patio look ties together the cabinets and walls without drawing all the attention to itself.

Photographs by Andre Aloshine, Aloshine Imagery

Jozef Custom Ironworks, Inc.

Bridgeport, Connecticut

"There is nothing quite like the Old World charm of hand-wrought iron and bronze with distinctive, extraordinary styles and exceptional quality."

—Jozef Witkowski

ABOVE: We chose a materials palette of black satin-finished wrought iron for the railing and bronze for the moulding and finial, giving the stairway a timelessly elegant aesthetic.

FACING PAGE: The custom bronze interior railing's patina finish is ideal for showcasing the engaging array of curvilinear and rectilinear forms, which dance in and around the stabilizing squared motif.
Photographs by Jozef Custom Ironworks, Inc.

"Exceptional ironwork enhances living and work spaces, including outdoor areas, through the thoughtful incorporation of creatively designed and painstakingly handcrafted pieces."

—Jozef Witkowski

RIGHT: Elegant and inviting, the arched iron garden gate with lantern features a painted black finish and is simply charming.

FACING PAGE LEFT: Sculptural in every way, the stunning bronze candelabra with a gilded finish would be the consummate centerpiece to any special space.

FACING PAGE TOP: A finely crafted table element met the owner's desire for a very tactile, three-dimensional design, which features bronze with a two-tone patina.

FACING PAGE BOTTOM: Beautiful leaves ornament a winsome wine cellar door that is iron with a brushed metal finish.
Photographs by Jozef Custom Ironworks, Inc.

"Whether carving, bookmatching, or resawing, woodwork is about understanding the unique characteristics of the material—the right wood and approach for the desired aesthetic."

—Budd Kelley

ABOVE: Our work incorporates every element: lighting, ceiling patterns, and architecture. From a warm and comforting study with built-ins to curved and radius work in a luxury powder room, we take every detail into consideration.

FACING PAGE: Rich and strong, our woodwork reflects the expectations of the homeowners we work with. The finished wood of an arched, curved design gives built-ins a commanding presence. Sturdy and defined, the head of the pediment shows solid craftsmanship.
Photographs by Sam Gray

"It isn't just about running a company—we're part of a community. That's why our affiliation with groups like the Architectural Woodwork Institute is so important."

—Jeff Burton

TOP & BOTTOM: When a contractor said that constructing an intricate changing table was proving troublesome, we took the challenge. The beautiful piece shows off round bookmatching, raised panels, and alternating grain patterning. One-of-a-kind and built to stand out, the changing stand sits in the master suite of a luxury New England home.

FACING PAGE: Plush and welcoming, the room of a private residence integrates storage with aesthetics. The deep-hued bookcases complement the ceiling's intense blue tones to create a relaxed setting.

Photographs by Peter Bart

"Handcrafted artisan tile transforms everyday rooms into vibrant, inspiring living spaces."

—Kristin Powers

ABOVE: To maintain the simple, elegant feel in the master bathroom without becoming monotonous, we mixed a variety of tiles and patterns in similar colors—Fog and Milk White. The floor's smaller basket-weave pattern—part of our sheeted Elemental mosaic collection—naturally prevents slipping and complements the tub's larger tiles. We created a custom baseboard out of our Classic Highland Crown and flat field tile, then capped it with our Monadnock liner to break up the tub's classic subway pattern.

FACING PAGE: The vertical brick-bond mosaic pattern created a peaceful spa atmosphere that coordinated with the smooth slate provided by the designer. The tile is all glazed in Vermont Green, but the many inherent variations confer a rich, organic feel.

Photographs by Eric Roth

"Tile can serve as a focal piece or as a way to tie everything together; when you're lucky, it does both."

—Kristin Powers

ABOVE LEFT & RIGHT: To create a Zen-like ambience in both the steam bathroom and powder room, we installed one tile element on the walls. Glazed in either Outer Galaxy or Indian Red, the fascinating range of hues adds liveliness without being overbearing. In the steam bathroom where even the ceiling is tiled, we installed Sharkskin-glazed mosaics to augment the shower floor. While the powder room has a modern flair with the stacked tile pattern, the fiery color speaks of an earthy feel.
Photographs by Eric Roth

FACING PAGE TOP LEFT: The fountain renovation was intentionally designed with a myriad of sizes and colors in order to achieve a rich and lively dappled effect. All of our tiles are stoneware and can withstand constant immersion and a freeze-thaw environment.
Photograph by Kristin Powers

FACING PAGE TOP RIGHT: Our Big Skinny Brick creates a rustic, plank-like feel, while the warm Bamboo glaze enhances the room's organic peacefulness.
Photograph by Rob Karosis

FACING PAGE BOTTOM: The classic New England kitchen design required subtle colors, simple textures, and a clean, comfortable feel. We used our 1- by 4-inch bricks in Milk White and Sharkskin to unify the room while accentuating the other design elements.
Photograph by Eric Roth

"I love to work with people who open up their dreams and who trust that I will interpret them."

—Susan Symonds

ABOVE LEFT & RIGHT: Contributing to the calm atmosphere, the wall color and soft fabrics flow throughout the living room and highlight the wine tasting area. Perfect for entertaining, the swivel barstools supply additional seating for guests and family, a large upholstered sofa hugs the south and west sides of the room, and a low bench sits by the fireplace and faces a sofa, chairs, and glass-topped table. I designed the carpet, inspired by the computer-generated art, which unifies the space.

FACING PAGE: To utilize all of the house's small spaces, I designed a small and cushy built-in banquette for the alcove and placed it over the cabinet housing all the audiovisual equipment. The venting design on the side of the banquette was inspired by the art above and then echoed in the wall sconce and cabinet hardware. Offering flexibility for conversation, a Dakota Jackson chair floats in the space.

PREVIOUS PAGES: An architecturally renovated ranch-style 1950s house was reconfigured internally into a French-style retreat. French tiles accentuate the fireplace while elegant sconces and a convex sunburst mirror increase illumination in the light-filled space. Hardy fabrics add detail and texture that are perfect for a family-filled room, and the colorful juxtaposition accentuates the blue, yellow, and white palette. Bright red gerbera daisies in silver cups add just the right touch.

Photographs by Nat Rea

"Quality and comfort should be inherent in a space designed for real living."

—Susan Symonds

RIGHT: In a bright and comfortable sitting room perfect for reading, watching television, and playing games, a custom-designed sectional takes advantage of every inch of space available and has upholstered base drawers for storage. The two leather stools from Soane double as ottomans or additional seating, and their mushroom shape is in juxtaposition to the angular graphic shapes elsewhere. The beautiful wood cabinet cleverly houses a small refrigerator plus books and a subwoofer, and the mica shaded lamp sits on it as a piece of art and a source of light.
Photograph by Nat Rea

"The composition of objects creates personality, interest, and rhythm."

—Susan Symonds

ABOVE LEFT: Opening to the kitchen, the family room is used by the residents as a retreat as well as for entertainment. They wanted their existing inventory utilized in a new way, with three different zones—an informal dining area, a conversation area by the fireplace, and a space to accommodate major seating.

ABOVE RIGHT: Inspired to design a private sitting area to showcase a beautiful card table acquired by my client on a trip abroad, I took advantage of the niche to house classic statuary, designed the carpet, which complements the soft wall treatment in ombre finish by artist Peter Bailey, and added an elegant patterned curtain to add softness to the once-hollow space.

FACING PAGE: Paying homage to the home's fine history and architecture without being heavy and pretentious, a corner view of the ballroom—now the living room—of the Newport summer residence reveals the resident's love of color and modern grandeur. I designed the rug to visually anchor the deep-cushioned club chairs, French-style arm chairs covered in Bergamo fabrics, and contemporary glass piece by David Van Noppen.
Photographs by Nat Rea

"Wall color and the combination of hue, balance, and texture throughout the space establish the mood."

—Susan Symonds

ABOVE: Accommodating the residents' love of blue and white, we gave the master bedroom a facelift and incorporated matching porcelains into the color scheme. I created a private oasis with two seating areas—by the fireplace and in the arched alcove dressing room. Rich blue walls and curtains with swaged cornices accentuate the space's height and fine architectural details.

FACING PAGE TOP: In the main seating area of the apartment's living room, the creamy linen wall color establishes the mood while a few colorful pillows and the patterned fabric on the club chair and ottoman bring in just the right note. To take advantage of the view, I treated the windows very lightly with side panels and Austrian shades of lace by F. Schumacher & Company.

FACING PAGE BOTTOM LEFT: The entryway welcomes guests with colorful wallpaper, which sets the mood for the classical and color-infused living room. A desk stands ready for sorting mail and provides extra seating for arriving guests.

FACING PAGE BOTTOM RIGHT: For a client who loves to entertain and frequently has small groups over for a game of bridge, I created the soft palette and subtle patterns to complement the exquisite artwork. I collaborated with renowned artist Toots Zynsky, one of two American glass artists in the Louvre, and designed a pedestal to showcase her breathtaking commissioned glass piece.
Photographs by Nat Rea

"All elements conspire to create a home that is serene, understated, and welcoming."

—Susan Symonds

ABOVE: The resident wanted a library with warm but not heavy tones and liberal touches of deep blue. The custom millwork throughout is hand-rubbed, bookmatched, crotch mahogany inlay. Rich textures from Lee Jofa, Scalamandré, Brunschwig et Fils, and Zimmer + Rohde complement the Symonds-designed rug, which pulls the elements together to create the ultimate masculine retreat.

FACING PAGE TOP: Combining high-tech amenities with Old World charm and craftsmanship, the wine cellar can host wine tastings as well as elegant informal meals at the Portuguese table. Two portraits by Russian artist Arkipor provide a perfect backdrop.

FACING PAGE BOTTOM: Converted from a screened porch, the conservatory provides a light-filled respite from the stresses of the day. The custom-designed back-to-back settees enable this small space to have two distinct conversation areas. The room is perfect for entertaining as well reading a newspaper with morning coffee.
Photographs by Nat Rea

> "A rug is an heirloom painting on the floor."
>
> —Jerry Arcari

ABOVE: One end of an Arts-and-Crafts-style living room looks out onto the ocean; the other end views a saltwater pond. With space at a premium and a constant stream of traffic from children and a dog, an antique Sarouk rug circa 1920 blends artistically and is very forgiving.
Photograph by Peter Jaquith

FACING PAGE: For a fully decorated third-floor room, finding the perfect rug to tie the fine design elements together was critical. The Boston brownstone showcases original Audubon bird prints, Murano glass chandeliers, and custom hand-carved furniture from Italy. The 19th-century Serapi rug beautifully provides a depth of color to the soft tones and fine furniture.
Photograph by James Abst

ABOVE: A new Oushak rug from Turkey mimics ancient designs. The soft blue, salmon, and camel colors set the tone for an elegant yet informal dining room by the sea.
Photograph by Eric Roth

LEFT: To coordinate a modern breakfast room in Gloucester with the blue-green of the outside environment, we designed our exclusive Panel Fish rug. Large-scale fish and square panels blend perfectly with the straight lines of the furniture and the ocean views.
Photograph by Michael Naimo

FACING PAGE TOP: For a well-used media and family room in Watch Hill, Rhode Island, the homeowner's designer, William Hullsman, created a design that imitates the pattern left in the sand after a wave recedes. The wool and silk rug crafted in Nepal interacts smoothly with the blue of the ocean and the upholstery in the Art Deco-inspired furniture.
Photograph by Eric Roth

FACING PAGE BOTTOM: A third-floor attic getaway room with an eyelid window view of the sea required a rug that reflected its simple palette of cream and blue. The vegetable-dyed Peshawar rug featuring a transitional design beckons the homeowners to relax.
Photograph by Eric Roth

"Fall in love with a rug; then build a room around the design."

—Jerry Arcari

"Each rug is an incredible art form created by talented craftspeople."
—Jerry Arcari

ABOVE: The gentle tones of the Egyptian rug with a subtle dragon Oushak design blend well with the soft tones throughout the main living room. The rug's hues, its wide borders, and the room's large-scale elements all contribute to the aura of relaxation.
Photograph by Eric Roth

FACING PAGE TOP: We connected various elements, such as the handcrafted fireplace tiles, modern art, a painted coffee table, and a balcony sea view, through the blue color and the repetitive starfish design of the Wilton-weave broadloom carpet.
Photograph by Eric Roth

FACING PAGE BOTTOM: A staircase provides an excellent area to introduce additional interest. For a formal curved location, Axminster-weave staircase carpeting in royal blue pinpoint design with a repeating star border highlights the natural wood. For a more visually choppy area, a continuous hall and stair runner in natural sisal unites the space. A blue linen binding provides a crisp edge.
Left photograph by Michael Naimo
Right photograph by Eric Roth

"The rug craft is an intricate process, from the picking of plants for the dye to the hand-knotting of the wool."

—Jerry Arcari

ABOVE LEFT: A historic Greek Revival house in Salem, Massachusetts, called for a formal and strong visual impact. The burgundy Axminster carpeting with an intricate border was crafted on a power loom to fit the narrow space and then continue on the landing. We had artist Andrea Sweeney paint the adjacent historically appropriate mural.
Photograph by Peter Jaquith

ABOVE RIGHT: Framed by a Southern pine floor, the wool and mohair Oushak rug echoes the blue of the ocean outside the master bedroom.
Photograph by Eric Roth

FACING PAGE: When the Labrador retriever is not the focal point, a large salmon medallion in the Oushak rug centers the entry hall in Watch Hill, Rhode Island. The warm colors and design invite visitors into the home and aid in the circulation between the living and dining rooms and the staircase to the second floor.
Photograph by David Roth

"Silk infuses a rug with a slight punch."

—Jerry Arcari

RIGHT: A homeowner in Massachusetts requested we design a Tibetan-weave rug to fit the exact dimensions for the living room and to blend with the room's various elements. We created our Sea of Treasure design in wool and silk as a modern foundation for the more traditional furniture and accessories.
Photograph by Eric Roth

FACING PAGE TOP: We selected striped Missoni carpeting to emphasize the linearity of the third-floor guest room and maintain a beach-like aesthetic. The stripes play off the dust ruffles; the lime-green border highlights the pillows.
Photograph by David Roth

FACING PAGE BOTTOM LEFT: The all-over floral design of the Tibetan-weave, wool and silk rug from Nepal creates a feeling of natural softness and elegance. Gentle grey-greens and soft blue emanate a quiet mood in the second-floor bedroom in Watch Hill, Rhode Island.
Photograph by David Roth

FACING PAGE BOTTOM RIGHT: White imported marble and gold fixtures are prominent design elements in a modern spa bathroom in Boston. The ivory border in the tribal rug blends with the marble while the blue coordinates with the accessories and adjoining dressing area walls. The lush Persian mountain wool of the Gabbeh runner is gentle to bare feet.
Photograph by James Abst

Lux Lighting Design

"Light is an ethereal energy. It is, unequivocally, the most crucial element in an environment. Natural light is my inspiration."

—Doreen Le May Madden

ABOVE: As founder and principal of my firm, my passion for lighting is evident in each project, which has resulted in many new referrals. My understanding of how light will play with architecture as well as the psychological and physiological effects of light result in a custom lighting scheme that fulfills my clients' every need. In this Cape Cod home, perfectly placed lighting shows off the careful, contemporary architecture. A trussed ceiling detail is silhouetted and highlighted simultaneously. Without any uplighting, these trusses would disappear under nightfall. With limited wall space, strategically placed sconces simulate a natural reflectance of light throughout the space, providing a comfortable, yet somewhat dramatic lighting effect.
Photograph by Brian Vanden Brink

FACING PAGE: In a neighborhood where curb appeal is expected, a home setting is to attract the eye of passersby, whether it's day or night. To achieve that, small pools of light instead of large washes were used. The lighting scheme leads viewers' eyes to the most appealing elements of the home and creates a welcoming atmosphere.
Photograph by Brett Drury

"The relationship of light and shadow has amazing visual possibilities to intensify shape."

—Doreen Le May Madden

ABOVE: The value of hiring a professionally trained lighting designer is clear to those who are knowledgeable of their services. The International Association of Lighting Designers, Illuminating Engineering Society of North America, and the NCQLP are important organizations to use as a resource, as they empower homeowners to commission wisely. A combination of lighting design techniques turns a master suite into a soothing retreat using varying intensities and angles of light. Although a chandelier serves as the focal point, the seating area and topiaries grab attention with the help of recessed lighting; cove lighting adds to the room's ease. This particular lighting scene is one of many that Lux programmed in the lighting control system.

FACING PAGE: A grand space demands the lighting designer's control—with so much room, the eye needs direction. As a professionally certified lighting designer, I bring formal training and artistry to each project. With light as a guide, one's eye is led from the ceiling and follows the path of illumination down to the sitting area, creating a more intimate scale. Recessed and integrated lighting in coves and millwork highlights various elements to create a more intimate space. Antique sconces deserve special attention, skillfully placed on either side of the gilded mirror, above the fireplace, and between the room's windows.
Photographs by Sam Gray

"Energy-efficient lighting doesn't equate to an aesthetic sacrifice. Creatively using the latest technology in your lighting plans can lend itself to a sophisticated lighting design; don't assume you cannot have the best of both worlds."

—Doreen Le May Madden

RIGHT: With the goal of accentuating a private crystal collection, we detailed integrated lighting: sidelighting and toplighting to fully articulate the collection. By ensuring the light sources were hidden from view, thus being free of glare, viewers can easily be drawn to the display and fully enjoy each object.
Photograph by Brett Drury

FACING PAGE TOP: High ceilings can require very different lighting techniques. For this trussed family room, I wanted to emphasize the details and refrain from using overbearing lights due to the various activities the client was planning on for this room. To achieve that, I created details for lighting troughs within the trusses, essentially creating a light fixture from the truss itself. The result is the accentuation of the beams with lighting that provides an overall appeal for general uses in the room. Another living room, with 16-foot ceilings, possessed a multitude of textures that deserved attention. The client preferred a clean lighting scheme with no decorative element that would interfere with planned-for dramatic artwork. In order to give the room its most flattering look and underscore the fireplace, hearth, and fabric, I used recessed lighting with various intensities of light sources and programmed the control system to provide many lighting scenes I felt the client would desire.
Photographs by Sam Gray and Brett Drury

FACING PAGE BOTTOM: A coffered-ceiling library needed the perfect lighting strategy to show off its rich woods and deep colors. Decorative sconces provide a focal point. Integrated lighting in mouldings and recessed downlighting highlight the textures in the space. The use of warm white light sources give the room its personality and ambience. Books, furniture, and craftwork become the highlights of the space while providing required task lighting.
Photograph by Sam Gray

CATHY GERSON STUDIOS

Southborough, Massachusetts

"I feel like a kid at Christmas each time I open my kiln. When designing, I allow my instinct to guide me and I just go for it."

—Cathy Gerson

ABOVE: For a seaside home, I crafted a 7-foot by 4-foot, three-dimensional, three-section mural to reflect what the homeowner saw outside her window. I designed the left side straight and kept the right side open-ended so the ocean scene would feel more alive, as if it were being born from the wall. The negative space of the wall helps define the three portions of the image—the sky, the water, and the earth.

FACING PAGE: Each project begins with a rendering of the design that I adjust to account for clay shrinkage in the kiln. The pieces are hand-cut, numbered, and fit together like a giant puzzle. The many electrical outlets made designing and hand-cutting the ceramic backsplash tiles a complex process. Creating the colors to blend with the existing countertop and Oriental rug was a fun challenge.

Photographs by Cathy Gerson

"I love working with clay because of its tactile nature and because, even after years of experience, I'm still learning new techniques to manipulate the material."

—Cathy Gerson

LEFT: During a trip to Turkey, the ancient ruins and hieroglyphics spurred my interest in foreign culture. I hand-carved individual tiles to create a 42-inch-tall obelisk, which would also lend itself nicely to a larger piece of sculpture, such as columns.
Photograph by Jonathan Wallen

FACING PAGE LEFT: Everyday objects provide great inspiration for artistic tile murals. A New England quilt motivated me to imagine a tile quilt. Peruvian rugs piqued a fascination with concave and convex lines and I translated that into an intricate pattern. Even dinosaur bones influenced the design of straight floating objects on a static background.
Top photograph by Steve Lee
Middle photograph by Karen Bernhardt
Bottom photograph by Lisa Sacks

FACING PAGE RIGHT: I love abstract art, so I immediately pictured a specific style when I was asked to design a mural based on a '54 DeSoto. I hung the 3-foot by 2-and-a-half-foot mural in a metal frame to allow for versatile uses.
Photograph by Cathy Gerson

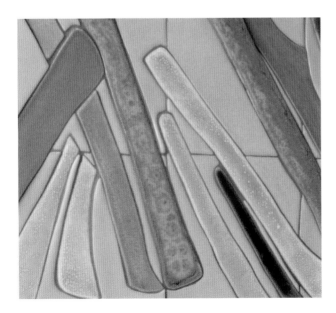

D SCALE

"Scale, proportion, comfort, and glamour. It all merges here."

—Dennis Duffy

ABOVE: National and international art pieces come together. We collect accessories that range from Indonesian pillows to Italian glassware, as well as our own designs that utilize elemental components like leather and glass.

FACING PAGE: Vignettes within our studio help people get an idea of what they like and what will work in their homes. All of our work is tailored to the individual—we are a true boutique. Constantly pulling in a wide range of materials, our portfolio begins with the D Scale Collection, a combination of sculptural shapes and sensual finishes. The Bette sofa and Geena chair sit amongst two bone tables, one revealing a smooth surface and the other a rough façade. This juxtaposition draws attention to the distinct variations of the furniture. Featured on the coffee table is a glass piece by Amanda Brisbane, the UK's foremost sand-casted glass artist.
Photographs by Michael Lee

"My designs convey sensuality and modernism without feeling fragile. These elements are meant to enjoy."

—Dennis Duffy

ABOVE: After living in New York and settling in Boston, I understand the need for small-space flexibility. Furniture should raise your ability to function in a room, not hinder it, regardless of its size. A modern take on the tuxedo-style sofa, the Simon sofa adds a plush, sensual tone to the room. Directly in front of that sits a 48-inch square table, designed to conform to intimate spaces. Cantilevered with a lower shelf, the table features an open back half that stores a sleek leather bench. The chair comes from Argentina and sits next to a mahogany table with a floating glass top, adding contemporary originality to the setting.
Photograph by Chris Vaccaro

FACING PAGE TOP & MIDDLE: Simple, yet sculptural, our pieces show amazing versatility. Placing them in either a modern aesthetic or in an antique setting works well, letting the client define the piece in their own right. A core collection table lets the softness of its shape come through, even though it expresses strong, definitive lines. The Bette sofa fits beautifully into nearly any interior with its rich neutral tones and classic appeal.
Photographs by Michael Brzoza

FACING PAGE BOTTOM: A really great design speaks for itself—and a 1950s Italian chair discovered in Buenos Aires is no exception. This would make a striking addition to any collection.
Photograph by Michael Brzoza

"Copper is a fantastic material—it has incredible longevity yet it can be molded into almost any shape imaginable."

—Erin Bluteau

ABOVE: The art studio owner and architect wanted a material that over time would age nicely and portray the effect of being nestled in the woods—almost as if the studio were a sculpture itself. We blended 24-ounce copper sheets on the façade with a built-in copper gutter and copper diamond-shaped shingles. Over the course of three years, the copper has aged naturally to a beautiful patina.

FACING PAGE: Appearing as a portal into the hillside, the pumphouse door was designed with a wood core and multiple laminated panels. To keep the door watertight, each panel is locked together by hand-planished recessed channels. We used a special technique when applying the patina to make the door blend with the landscape.
Photographs by Erin Bluteau

"The simple beauty of copper changes the entire dynamic of the surrounding décor or design."

—Erin Bluteau

ABOVE: We polished Revere FreedomGrey™ copper to a high brilliance and then cut refined edges to fit within the mahogany doorframe. A ³⁄₈-inch bronze plate was waterjetted and polished before being installed. By merging these muted colors with a ruby red stained glass, the door provides an amazing focal point. A local artist crafted the bronze door handle.

FACING PAGE TOP: In a cottage-meets-modern home on Lake Champlain, the homeowner wanted a unique twist for her powder room vanity. We created a sturdy stainless steel frame and posts, shaped the copper around the frame, and crafted embossed recessions, cornice trim, and seamless corners. A dark bronze finish and a clear topcoat coordinate with the granite vanity and wood floor.

FACING PAGE BOTTOM: We created a beautifully aging, functional piece of art according to the architect's desire for the grill to appear as if it were part of the stone wall. We used TIG welding, an arc welding process that uses a nonconsumable tungsten electrode to produce the weld, on each seam of the 32-ounce copper and applied a light antique finish.
Photographs by Erin Bluteau

"People are often fooled into thinking that they hate curtains— and I love proving them wrong. Simple and understated, window designs have come a long way."

—Karen Gilman

ABOVE: Often, homeowners shy away from using rich colors in their curtain design. But when done properly, color simply adds warmth. Reeded wood rods hold deep coral curtains on gold leaf hardware in a formal Beacon Hill townhouse. The setting maintains a very traditional look without overpowering the fresh, youthful feel.
Photograph by Brantley Photography

FACING PAGE: When a couple was adamantly opposed to curtains, I made it a point to change their minds. By the end of it, we had installed treatments in the master bedroom, dining room, living room, and even the children's rooms. Now the spaces would seem empty without them. The curtains accent a unique art piece in the room, lying between the windows. Reclaimed from the Boston subway after its renovation, an old cloth Metro sign adorns the wall, turning memorabilia into art.
Photograph by Eric Roth

"With roots based in the old school aesthetic, I know that a designer's job is to account for the endless variables, but make it appear effortless in the end."

—Karen Gilman

ABOVE LEFT & RIGHT: In order to create the sense of a traditional, yet refreshing room, we used refined colors and clean lines. White undercurtains lie beneath the exterior fabric like an elegant petticoat and give the appearance of a breeze blowing through the room, even though the windows are closed.
Photographs by Brantley Photography

FACING PAGE TOP LEFT: When a Boston designer participated in a Palm Beach Red Cross showhouse, we wanted to create a long, lean appearance with the windows—a nod to Japanese design. To do so, we pulled out the room's crown moulding and achieved the precise look we were going for. We also created contour-cut pillows to accent the space and tie the room together.
Photograph by Brantley Photography

FACING PAGE TOP RIGHT: In a room with 10 full windows, the daily routine of opening and closing the curtains becomes a small commitment, which is why the space is an ideal candidate for automated treatments. After working on a couple's residence in Lexington, we designed their vacation home in Spring Lake, New Jersey. They provided a palette for me to work with and I chose the hand—or texture—of the fabric. This working relationship represents what we strive for with each project: a spirit of collaboration.
Photograph by Sam Gray

FACING PAGE BOTTOM: I began my own business at 25 and I've learned that there's no such thing as a small detail. Everything counts. In a home with dedicated equestrians, we designed a minimal, relaxed setting to match the homeowners' personalities and show off their art selections. The room offers a certain level of humility with its simplicity, a feat that requires a great deal of attention to achieve. We once again removed the crown moulding and designed the curtains to break for the floor at precisely the right moment. Not too much yet not too little, the room has a flawless ease to it.
Photograph by Eric Roth

Fire & Ice Studio | Deborah Goldhaft Design

Pawtucket, Rhode Island

"A sense of transformation is involved in working with any sort of glass. It is both solid and liquid simultaneously, moving and still, clear becoming opaque."

—Deborah Goldhaft

ABOVE: Implementing nontraditional sandblast techniques, I deep carved and etched three layers on both sides of 12- by 18-inch clear plate glass to mimic the ebb and flow patterns that water leaves in sand. These are the same patterns created by wind in desert sand dune formations. The art evokes a global implication of the earth's continuity through time with cycles coming and going.
Photograph by Press Pause Photography

FACING PAGE: Plate glass and mirror lend themselves to geometric imagery and light play. On a 15-inch double-sided etched plate glass mirror, I created a feeling of potential with a glimpse of future possibilities.
Photograph by Deborah Goldhaft

"I often feel like Alice in *Through the Looking Glass*—there is always a sense of wonder and surprise as each creation unveils itself to me."

—Deborah Goldhaft

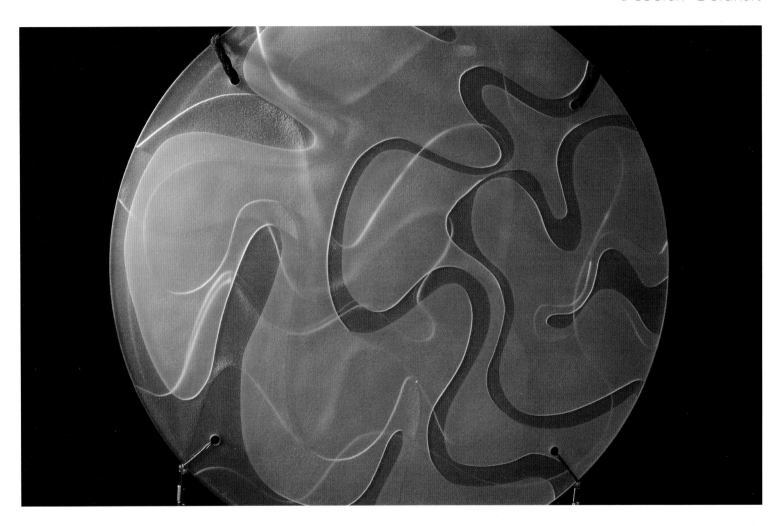

ABOVE: I deep carved three layers into both sides of a ¼-inch-thick clear plate disk with an estuary pattern based on the tides moving in and out. The three-dimensional artwork is expressed through its tactile quality and visual depth.
Photograph by Deborah Goldhaft

FACING PAGE TOP: A multilayer, three-dimensional tabletop incorporates feng shui principles with maple leaves and heron imagery.
Photograph by Deborah Goldhaft

FACING PAGE BOTTOM LEFT: I used mirror panels to reflect exterior light and exhibit backlit imagery of generic Native American symbols. The bronze and regular plate mirrors display double-sided designs that offer a second image when not lit.
Photograph by Deborah Goldhaft

FACING PAGE BOTTOM RIGHT: Through three, double-side etched, 15-inch plate glass rounds on a custom lit base, I formulated depth through space and time simultaneously. The design shows continental drift starting with the ancient supercontinent and ending 50 million years in our future.
Photograph by Roger Schreiber

Jeff Soderbergh Furniture | Sculpture | Design

Newport, Rhode Island

"I believe in preserving the history of our unique surroundings in a tangible way that can be passed down through the generations."

—Jeff Soderbergh

ABOVE & FACING PAGE: I begin a project by assessing both where and how the piece will be used. For the table, the homeowner appreciated Craftsman and Japanese-influenced style and loved the ocean. He desired a serene but sturdy homework area for two girls. I used pieces of a 19th-century copper roof from a Newport mansion that had a fantastic original patina from years of weathering and inlaid the copper into local windfall walnut.

Photographs by David Hansen Photography

ABOVE: The Dublin Bed was an amazing commission by a spiritually grounded U.S. Navy commander and his wife who, on a visit to the studio, fell in love with a late 19th-century gothic church window from Dublin. I incorporated their hand-forged iron scrolls and, to honor their travels to Japan, pieces of Japanese water glass.
Photograph by David Hansen Photography

FACING PAGE TOP: I transformed a reclaimed blacksmith sign cornice circa 1760 in Chestnut Hill, Pennsylvania, into an elegant side table that melds into graceful, Vermont maple legs.
Photograph by Bill Durvan

FACING PAGE MIDDLE: As soon as I found the 375-pound steel-clad fire door from the 1906 Jefferson Mill in Worcester, Massachusetts, I knew the family with the self-described unruly boys would love this as a table set in southern heart pine and Douglas fir beams circa 1875.
Photograph by David Hansen Photography

FACING PAGE BOTTOM: An 1880 Victorian cast steel heat grate sparked my interest to craft a Japanese-style tea table. Set atop hand-rubbed Honduran mahogany, the grate rests at the perfect height to kneel and drink tea.
Photograph by David Hansen Photography

FACING PAGE RIGHT: Built to complement the Dublin Bed, the side tables were quite challenging because the 150-year-old leaded glass windows had been warped through the years by the elements. I had to build unique forms for each window to follow the curve and then ensure the tables wouldn't appear disproportionate.
Photograph by David Hansen Photography

"Surface design is a discovery process of understanding the homeowner's personality, sensing the room's potential ambience, and tying all the surface elements together through color, pattern, and texture."

—Marilyn MacLeod

ABOVE: Trompe l'oeil, French for "fool the eye," is a painting technique that creates a realistic three-dimensional look on a two-dimensional surface. Color and shading produce volume, which are key to realism, while stylistic rendering prompts a unique appearance. The first two panels show the stylistic contrast between a formal look with tight ochre brushstrokes over a red base, and a casual look with looser ochre brushstrokes over an almond base. The forest green wall is also painted using trompe l'oeil techniques and features a stone niche surrounding a planted urn in a natural earth-tone palette.
Left & middle photographs by Jay Penni Photography
Right photograph by Jean Donohue Photography

FACING PAGE: A dreamy metallic plaster containing gold and silver mica flakes was hand troweled to provide a soft backdrop for a formal entrance. Because the room receives minimal sun exposure, the shimmering mica flakes capture and reflect additional light.
Photograph by David Snow Photography

"Eclectic styles, when blended correctly, are the most interesting designs because, like a mosaic, they reflect each family member's individuality and together form an integrated style."

—Marilyn MacLeod

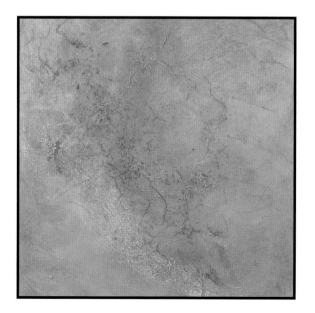

LEFT: I like to use traditional paint techniques in a modern way. For example, a subtle beauty can be achieved in a "lost and found" technique by layering and blending two different hues of yellow-green and blue-grey metallic plaster over a raised stencil of turquoise Venetian plaster. Design elements can be used singularly or repeated and combined to form structured or random patterns for an infinite number of design possibilities. The second panel shows how traditional paint techniques, such as gold leafing and antiquing, when done using an ancient pattern, can give an old concept a modern twist. The final panel shows how a crackled bright yellow Venetian plaster is toned down with brown glaze and infused with a subtle elegance by a thin veil of mica wax, which makes the old new again.
Photographs by Jay Penni Photography

FACING PAGE: A textured sand-like wall finish was chosen by Pamela Copeman Design Group to add warmth and comfort to the kitchen ambience. The blend of warm yellows with hints of pale blues and the gritty sand particles in the finish harmonize well with the smooth wood tones, iron hardware, and rich textiles in both the kitchen and the adjoining rooms.
Photograph by Jean Donohue Photography

"Designers drive the process. They have the unique ability to bring interior spaces up to a level beyond that of architecture. The goal is always fresh tracks in new snow, the evolution of signature style."

—Daryl Evans

ABOVE: The center table features a sunburst figured walnut top supported by a fluted column, complete with gilded trim. Table leafs allow for expansion if desired. Table design by William Hodgins, Inc.

FACING PAGE: We collaborated with the interior designer to create a Regency desk for a Boston penthouse. Details such as the antique leather top with blind tooling and gilded brass mouldings and mounts make the mahogany desk more decorative than functional. Overlooking a magnificent view of the city, it's the perfect spot for writing postcards. Desk design by William Hodgins, Inc.

Photographs by Richard Hulme

"Science can put a man on the moon but sooner or later he'll need a table. That's a job we'll definitely bid on."

—Richard Hulme

ABOVE: Constructed from walnut and yew wood with gold leaf gilded trim, a gentleman's study takes inspiration from an antique French bibliothèque. A triple band of mouldings establishes the architrave for the floor-to-ceiling paneling, giving the space a regal, yet warm feel. Study design by Saffron House, Inc.

FACING PAGE TOP: A traditional multiuse wall unit reaches 11 feet toward the ceiling, as it serves as a desk, an entertainment center, and a storage piece. Bifold doors in the center mask a flat-screen television, while a drop-down lid camouflages a workspace and the bottom compartments conceal media equipment. Carefully placed ventilation and wire passage were key in the design, which features oak with an antique limed finish. Wall unit design by John Berenson Interior Design.

FACING PAGE BOTTOM: Crystal display cabinets outfitted with antique mirror and antique leaded glass accented by silver-leaf caming illuminate the corner of a Boston brownstone. The built-in pieces reach 10 feet, as they feature marble tops and crotch mahogany panels. Cabinet design by Dell Mitchell Architects and Manuel de Santaren Interior Design.

Photographs by Richard Hulme

"The feel of the fabric and the tactile element of quilting furnish a sensation found in no other activity."

—Ann Lainhart

ABOVE: Each Bargello quilt, which is crafted using straight strips of fabric in a mountain and valley style, portrays an incredible depth and movement within the design. I create the three-dimensional effect using various colors and sizes, and then incorporate curves into the design, as in the Jaws Off Center and the Sands of Time Off Center quilts, through the shifting colors. The off-center designs were challenging because I enjoy symmetry; the end result, though, rendered a unique image that stimulates the eye.

FACING PAGE: First used in needlepoint, Bargello designs date back to the Middle Ages in the Bargello Palace in Florence, Italy. For my unique interpretation, I organize the material into groups of eight fabrics within each color family and shift from one group to another. I also use only patterned fabric, as in the abstract color-shift Bargello quilt, so that the piece has interest up close as well as at a distance. *Photographs by Fredrick K. Bodin*

"The beginning of a quilt is like starting a journey that can lead into an infinite number of directions."

—Ann Lainhart

ABOVE: My personal challenge with the Color Rules quilt was to see how many fabrics I could incorporate in the nearly 4- by 5-foot wall hanging. In the end, more than 500 different fabrics took numerous hours to prepare into color families and then approximately three weeks to quilt together.
Photograph by Fredrick K. Bodin

FACING PAGE LEFT: The mariner's compass, an old quilt block technique, is popular because of the depth created from the appearance of different levels of points. By implementing the fussy-cut method—when a fabric is cut to isolate a specific motif—and then repeating that motif around the compass, I create a kaleidoscope design in the center. The exact result of the center design is always an exciting surprise.
Photographs by Charles R. Lynch

FACING PAGE RIGHT: The Red Lanterns quilt embodies the ultimate use of shades from one color family to create a three-dimensional feel. The beige tones in the background give the lantern-like image a rounded feel. My inspiration when creating this design stemmed from three areas: the look of Japanese lanterns, the movement of the wind spinners that are hung like chimes, and my love of geometric designs.
Photograph by Fredrick K. Bodin

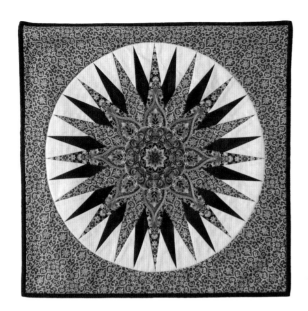

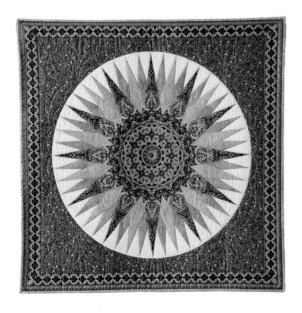

H. KEITH WAGNER

Burlington, Vermont

"Art, as with landscape architecture, is about the tactile qualities of the materials, and this invites people to engage with the piece."

—Keith Wagner

ABOVE: Found scrap metal like railroad spikes, wire cable, and cold-rolled steel are used to create sculpture with a warm russet color and varied textures.
Photographs by Jim Westphalen

FACING PAGE: At a modern upstate New York residence, spheres were crafted out of old mortar pans and incorporated into a sculpture garden. In one sphere, a one-inch slot allows a light inside to softly illuminate from within the artwork and adds a dramatic effect as guests walk toward the house.
Photograph by Keith Wagner

Hayden Hillsgrove Stone Masonry, page 235   H. Keith Wagner Partnership, page 251

living the elements

chapter five

Custom Pools, page 245

Studio B Designworks, page 265

Liquid Landscape Designs, page 257

HAYDEN HILLSGROVE STONE MASONRY

Moultonboro, New Hampshire

"There is nothing more symbolic of stonework than the stone arch."

—Michael Del Sesto

ABOVE & FACING PAGE: We always look to native stones first, and Villa Como is no different. Old York granite in the arch entry into the basement wine cellar complements the English-style pub design of the adjacent room. To maintain cohesiveness throughout the property, we incorporated the same granite in the undulating motions of the landscaping. Pavers and granite capping stones, supplied by White Mountain Stone Company, were also blended into the design to complement the Old York granite.

Photographs by Rixon Photography LLC

ABOVE & FACING PAGE: We worked in conjunction with the architect and landscape architect to create an infinity-edge pool with a waterfall and swim-in grotto. We hid a concrete structure behind the stone elements to ensure the grotto blended with the landscape. New York limestone lended itself well for the walls of the grotto and on the ledge because of its stalactite feel. For the grotto ceiling, a synthetic material was more appropriate for its lighter weight, so we had an artist carve joint lines and add color to match the natural stone. One of the most important components of this project was the outstanding team. It was truly a collaborative effort. Designers, craftsmen, and suppliers, such as White Mountain Stone Company who supplied the granite pool paving, capstones, and steps, helped to make the project successful.

Photographs by Michael Del Sesto

"The use of stone can ground a project and make it feel a part of the natural landscape."

—Michael Del Sesto

TOP & BOTTOM: At the Villa Como project, the large patio creates interesting visuals. The hidden view on the steps provides an element of surprise, and the sweeping turns of the cabana and patio edge offer soft boundaries. We continued with the Old York granite on the stair walls and around the cabana, then incorporated Old Gold granite for the steps and Autumn Gold granite for the patio stone, all provided by White Mountain Stone Company.

FACING PAGE: Developing a harmony with the stones, architecture, and landscape is important in stonework. On the columns, we used Old York granite to anchor the roof structure and then used Old Gold granite paving to highlight the sweeping shingle flair as it meets the patio. The seamless transition from the residence into the landscape and other stones is evident in how the various stones in the veneer, window sills, and headers complement each other and seem to spring forth from the ground.
Photographs by Rixon Photography LLC

"Through texture, color, and placement, good stonework should evoke a certain emotion."

—Michael Del Sesto

ABOVE: We designed and ordered precisely cut architectural granite from White Mountain Stone for this gatehouse. We then installed it to blend well with the native fieldstone and hand-carved maple leaf tablets.

RIGHT: Using numerous pieces of internationally sourced Old Gold granite that were hand carved to fit the top of a chimney, we were able to achieve the designer's goals and stay within budget.

FACING PAGE TOP: Even with two different types of residential architecture, the native fieldstone's round shape provides a soft image with impressive depth due to the stone's textures and contours. This shape helps to tone down large, hard architectural elements.

FACING PAGE BOTTOM: Stonework can often be very personal for a homeowner. For a fireplace, the homeowner collected stones from her local beach nearly every day. With her involvement, we patterned them together like a puzzle and helped create something that she felt intimately involved in. We used a piece of reclaimed Rockport granite for the mantel.
Photographs by Michael Del Sesto

"Whether using rounded fieldstone or angular granite, the key is to accentuate the natural features of each stone through the joinery work."

—Michael Del Sesto

LEFT: We integrated complementary stones that had a lot of presence and that would appear aged—granite from Maine and New Hampshire for the veneer and ledge, and Canadian granite for the window sill and caps.

FACING PAGE TOP: Collaboration with architects, designers, and other professionals on a project is critical to the success, especially for an estate house with 31,000 square feet. We wanted to combine the Old World imagery with new architecture by incorporating elements like arches and window detail from White Mountain Stone. We constructed the numerous fountains out of a precast material that mimicked real stone.

FACING PAGE BOTTOM: Water interjected into the landscape always adds a nice, tranquil atmosphere. The homeowners wanted a waterfall effect, so we split reclaimed railroad bridge blocks to the necessary sizes and shapes to create the dams on the upper and lower level. The lower waterfall was created using one large stone that was cut to feature steps for a walkway.

Photographs by Michael Del Sesto

"A water feature, especially a hot tub, can help reinvigorate the spirit, both mentally and physically."

—Brian Short

ABOVE & FACING PAGE: Following the architect's design, we built a contemporary structure with a new style that blended with the home's numerous arches. The 70-foot-long vanishing edge of the pool, which requires a perfectly level construction, extended the visual appeal toward the ocean for a dramatic view. A circular, raised spa adds a central feature that anchors the arch details.
Photographs by Deeds Johnson

"Using gunite allows the imagination to be brought to life through the shape of a pool."

—Brian Short

LEFT: Created so the homeowner could entertain or just sit back and relax, the simple yet sophisticated backyard incorporates a traditional rectangular pool that has some of the most luxurious amenities. The numerous features in the heated, low-maintenance, saltwater pool include an automatic safety cover, granite lions that emanate streams of water, a six-foot sheer descent waterfall from a bench, a corner hot tub, a white river rock plaster finish, and a cantilever edge.

FACING PAGE: To provide a place for a family to enjoy, we built a pool with numerous waterfalls, each at the temperature of either the pool or spa. We added a marble table and bench in the shallow end along with a bridge over to the cabana. A river rock finish on the floor of the pool and a stone diving rock integrate the natural environment into the space.

Photographs by Deeds Johnson

"The sign of a true craftsman is when new landscaping blends beautifully with the existing nature."

—Brian Short

ABOVE & FACING PAGE: The pool's swooping curves and cascading water present a backyard paradise overlooking one of Boston's premier golf courses. To accommodate a 50-foot-tall hill, we designed a vanishing edge to cascade down over the sloped natural stone tile into a smaller pool at the bottom. Dark accent stone, which mirrors the dark river rock on the floor of the pool, interrupts the tiled wall and adds depth.

Photographs by Deeds Johnson

H. KEITH WAGNER PARTNERSHIP

"The house took a seat where the site offered a chair."

—Keith Wagner

ABOVE & FACING PAGE: The 11-inch-caliper honey locust tree and an entry garden of perennials and ornamental grasses create a warm entry experience to the home. On the lakeside, the geometry of the curved stairway guides guests down 8-inch-thick bluestone slab steps to a raised, curved boardwalk leading to the beach. On the stairway, local South Bay quartzite effuses a soft, buff color that is warm and complements the architect's selection for cedar siding.
Photographs by Jim Westphalen

"Variety in texture and subtle changes of hue in the landscape make for a more interesting composition."

—Keith Wagner

ABOVE & FACING PAGE: The pool terrace of bluestone was sited on the south side of the home to provide as much warmth and protection from the cool lake winds as possible. The existing woods were edited to create a park-like landscape with a carpet of lawn and mature trees. Birch trees act as a scrim to allow some privacy from the autocourt. The grill was integrated into the stone walls. Crisp detailing of materials create a clean look for the contemporary landscape.
Photographs by Jim Westphalen

"I like a design in which the new landscape seamlessly flows from the architecture into the existing site."

—Keith Wagner

ABOVE LEFT & RIGHT: Large Vermont panton stones in a gravel walk between the garage and house and a step ramp from the autocourt to the front door evoke the sense of the landscape as fluid—in essence flowing around the house. A dock-like feel was created by using galvanized steel with ipe decking while allowing the ramp to hover about a foot to 18 inches above grade. Native understory along with the honey locust trees gives a dappled sun-and-shade effect to the entry garden.

FACING PAGE: On one end of Shelburne Farms, a newly constructed home needed a landscape that merged the traditional feel of the architecture with a few modern touches. Bluestone was used throughout the project including pool coping, walks, and the large entertainment terrace. A bed of ornamental grass between the pool and the home allows for privacy. On the side of the house, layers of plant material soften the geometric house while 3-inch-thick bluestone caps add visual strength and a contemporary feel.
Photographs by Jim Westphalen

LIQUID LANDSCAPE DESIGNS

Carlisle, Massachusetts

"Good lighting is crucial to outdoor enjoyment, especially in the fall. It brings about the sense of a true outdoor room."

—Jay Bearfield

ABOVE LEFT: Our mosaic fountains by Rock Art Studios are perfect for all spaces, especially small areas, because they can fit the available space. The glass tile mosaics, which can be created with one of 12 standard images or can be completely customized with any image, were featured with the standard ornamental grass image for DIY Network's "Indoors Out" show.

ABOVE RIGHT & FACING PAGE: To accommodate a dramatic grade change, water flows next to the natural stone steps and cascades into a lower pond, as a bluestone ledge juts out to add a modern touch. The lighting became especially important to extend the outdoor entertaining season and to enhance indoor parties during the holidays as the light plays off of the ice in the watercourse.
Photographs by Ben Finn

"The beauty of water is that a large flow isn't always required to distract the human mind—a small, trickling stream can make a huge difference."

—Jay Bearfield

ABOVE: We incorporated a water feature into a more formal landscape, designed by Alden Landscape Design, with a clean-design fountain as the primary focus within the koi- and water lily-filled pool. The feature was tailored to blend in with a traditional New England home.
Photograph by Jay Bearfield

RIGHT: A nearly 40-foot-long pond course with a bluestone path leads visitors through a city backyard with an artistically maneuvering watercourse that passes between two of the steppers as a water rillway.
Photograph by Jay Bearfield

FACING PAGE LEFT: As part of a design that included a swimming pool, we worked with the pool contractor to match the visual water levels of the two features. By using native fieldstone and designing with the 15-foot existing grade, the waterfall was created to blend with the surrounding natural landscape.
Photograph by Ben Finn

FACING PAGE TOP: Shaded areas present the perfect spot for a water feature. Complete with mossy boulders and native ferns amidst a woodland garden, the stream course feels right at home.
Photograph by Jay Bearfield

FACING PAGE BOTTOM: We repurposed a pedestal urn as the lead point of a small pond to dramatically transform a small patio area with just enough noise to accent the outdoor living space.
Photograph by Jay Bearfield

P RODGERS LLC

"Pairing different plant textures together is tricky—sometimes similar styles work well, while other times contrasting colors and textures offer the ideal look."

—Pamela Rodgers

ABOVE & FACING PAGE: After a Jamestown Island house was renovated, only two large maples existed and there was virtually no circulation on the property. I needed to bring the landscape up to the scale of the home. From the carriage house, I designed a native fieldstone wall to guide guests onto the bluestone terrace, which overlooks the bay. The terrace, as well as a cozy firepit and relaxing Adirondack chairs, accommodates the homeowners' penchant for entertaining. Native bayberry, dogwoods, and beech trees with splashes of red-colored plants give the terrace a bit of privacy from the road and neighboring properties. The stone wall continues toward the house, where wraparound porches offer additional viewing areas of the bay.

Photographs by Marianne Lee

"Containers should blend into the surrounding landscape to allow the plants within them to be the main focus."

—Pamela Rodgers

TOP & BOTTOM: At a home in Providence, a bluestone walkway guides visitors through strolling gardens that include a perennial area with a water feature, a collection of roses, and a sunken garden. One segment meanders through a vegetable garden, which accommodates requests from the chef, and includes a mix of cabbage with edible flowers, tomatoes, cucumbers, peppers, and squashes. Along the front side of the conservatory, a small bed for seasonal color includes a trellis system along the brick wall for clematis to add interest to the occasionally transitioning bed.
Photographs by Angel Tucker

FACING PAGE: In an exposed location on the coast, I used subtropical plants and peach colors that blended with the stone façade of the home to soften the look of the bluestone patio and to create a more inviting entry. Plants, such as canna, coleus, lavender, mandevilla, and phormium, were not only chosen for their tolerance of harsh coastal conditions but also to bring lush splashes of color against the native planting beds.
Photographs by Marianne Lee

"Blending the old with the new achieves timelessness and comfort. My designs work around that premise."

—Stephen Bagley

ABOVE: For a Massachusetts home set on the coast, I designed a curved wall and fence with multiple purposes in mind. The fence had to maintain privacy and offer safety, while allowing full views of the ocean just beyond the property's perimeter. Green, lush perennials add to the aesthetic appeal of the fence and help soften the angular lot boundaries. Hand-cut granite elements used in the walls and pillars show off traditional stone-cutting techniques—a historically significant craft in this particular town.

FACING PAGE: Constantly combining the old with the new, I created a classic look that blends clean, contemporary lines with historically driven architecture. The landscape works with the home's traditional renovation to reveal a seamless look, as if the home looked exactly the same a century ago. However, modernity remains in full force, giving the homeowners resort-style luxury with an array of amenities.
Photographs courtesy of Studio B Designworks

"For cohesion and spatial harmony, material selection is critical. Natural stone, wood, and metal often yield the best results."

—Stephen Bagley

ABOVE: A smart, well-planned lighting scheme extends the usable hours of the swimming pool and patio while connecting the home with its outdoor spaces. Built-in lighting illuminates walkways and kitchen surfaces and appears strategically in landscape elements and well-crafted masonry. Ideal for entertaining, the outdoor space gains a welcoming, ambient feel with this lighting program.

FACING PAGE TOP LEFT: With the environment weighing on America's conscience, protecting existing flora has become increasingly important in my projects. Leaving two mature saucer magnolias—among other shrubs—intact, I designed the outdoor space with entertaining and privacy in mind. Xeriscaping principles were also used to create an eco-aware setting.

FACING PAGE MIDDLE LEFT: The backyard should blend leisure with luxury. A poolside terrace does just that, offering a resort-like setting that encourages casual dining—perfect for summer luncheons.

FACING PAGE BOTTOM LEFT: With multifunctional design elements at play, a spa offers a foot rinse area on this beachside property. The ornamental herb garden and indigenous stepping stones create an intimate niche and show off the character of the site.

FACING PAGE RIGHT: To achieve all-around balance, granite, bluestone, and slate were used in a variety of ways—each complementing one another.
Photographs courtesy of Studio B Designworks

perspectives
ON DESIGN

NEW ENGLAND TEAM
ASSOCIATE PUBLISHER: Laureen Edelson
GRAPHIC DESIGNER: Kendall Muellner
EDITOR: Jennifer Nelson
MANAGING PRODUCTION COORDINATOR: Kristy Randall

HEADQUARTERS TEAM
PUBLISHER: Brian G. Carabet
PUBLISHER: John A. Shand
EXECUTIVE PUBLISHER: Phil Reavis
DIRECTOR OF DEVELOPMENT & DESIGN: Beth Benton Buckley
PUBLICATION & CIRCULATION MANAGER: Lauren B. Castelli
SENIOR GRAPHIC DESIGNER: Emily A. Kattan
GRAPHIC DESIGNER: Ashley Rodges
MANAGING EDITOR: Rosalie Z. Wilson
EDITOR: Anita M. Kasmar
EDITOR: Michael McConnell
EDITOR: Sarah Tangney
EDITOR: Lindsey Wilson
PRODUCTION COORDINATOR: Maylin Medina
PRODUCTION COORDINATOR: Drea Williams
PROJECT COORDINATOR: Laura Greenwood
TRAFFIC COORDINATOR: Brandi Breaux
ADMINISTRATIVE MANAGER: Carol Kendall
ADMINISTRATIVE ASSISTANT: Beverly Smith
CLIENT SUPPORT COORDINATOR: Amanda Mathers

PANACHE PARTNERS, LLC
CORPORATE HEADQUARTERS
1424 Gables Court
Plano, TX 75075
469.246.6060
www.panache.com
www.panachedesign.com

index

THE PANACHE COLLECTION

CREATING SPECTACULAR PUBLICATIONS FOR DISCERNING READERS

Dream Homes Series
An Exclusive Showcase of the Finest Architects, Designers and Builders

Carolinas
Chicago
Coastal California
Colorado
Deserts
Florida
Georgia
Los Angeles
Metro New York
Michigan
Minnesota
New England
New Jersey

Northern California
Ohio & Pennsylvania
Pacific Northwest
Philadelphia
South Florida
Southwest
Tennessee
Texas
Washington, D.C.

Spectacular Homes Series
An Exclusive Showcase of the Finest Interior Designers

California
Carolinas
Chicago
Colorado
Florida
Georgia
Heartland
London
Michigan
Minnesota
New England

Metro New York
Ohio & Pennsylvania
Pacific Northwest
Philadelphia
South Florida
Southwest
Tennessee
Texas
Toronto
Washington, D.C.
Western Canada

Perspectives on Design Series
Design Philosophies Expressed by Leading Professionals

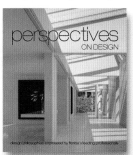

California
Carolinas
Chicago
Colorado
Florida
Georgia

Great Lakes
Minnesota
New England
Pacific Northwest
Southwest

Art of Celebration Series
The Making of a Gala

Chicago
Georgia
Midwest
New York
Philadelphia
South Florida
Southern California
Southwest
Texas
Washington, D.C.
Wine Country

Spectacular Wineries Series
A Captivating Tour of Established, Estate and Boutique Wineries

California's Central Coast
Napa Valley
New York
Sonoma County

Specialty Titles
The Finest in Unique Luxury Lifestyle Publications

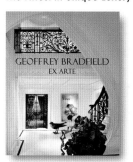

Cloth and Culture: Couture Creations of Ruth E. Funk
Distinguished Inns of North America
Extraordinary Homes California
Geoffrey Bradfield Ex Arte
Into the Earth: A Wine Cave Renaissance
Spectacular Golf of Colorado
Spectacular Golf of Texas
Spectacular Hotels
Spectacular Restaurants of Texas
Visions of Design

City by Design Series
An Architectural Perspective

Atlanta
Charlotte
Chicago
Dallas
Denver
Orlando
Phoenix
San Francisco
Texas

PanacheDesign.com
Where the Design Industry's Finest Professionals Gather, Share, and Inspire

PanacheDesign.com overflows with innovative ideas from leading architects, builders, interior designers, and other specialists. A gallery of design photographs and library of advice-oriented articles are among the comprehensive site's offerings.

PANACHE PARTNERS, LLC • 1424 GABLES COURT • PLANO, TEXAS 75075 • 469.246.6060 • WWW.PANACHE.COM